The Pattern
& The Glory

The New Testament
Pattern for the Glorious
End-Time Church

David Chapman

The Pattern & The Glory
David Chapman

TRU Publishing
P.O. Box 201
Thatcher, Arizona 85552

I would like to thank my wife Debbie for her faith and confidence in me when I needed it the most.

Table of Contents

Section One: Five-Fold Ministry & Pastoral Church Government

The Pattern and the Glory

God desires to fill His house with His glory. The glory only comes when divine order and pattern have been established. First the pattern, then the glory. It has always been this way. Moses received the pattern for the Tabernacle on the mount with God (Hebrews 8:5). Later, upon obedience to those instructions, God filled it with His glory. The same held true concerning the Tabernacle of David and the Temple of Solomon. When David tried to bring the Ark of God's presence to Zion without divine order, it met with judgment.

> **1 Chronicles 15:13 says: The LORD our God broke out against us, because we did not consult Him about the proper order.**

If God would only fill the type and "shadow of things to come" with His glory when divine order was established, how much more the antitype, the fulfillment of things to come – the Church. Does God expect us to be led on a lower level of order in the dispensation of the Holy Spirit than they were under the law? God wants to fill His house, but His house is no longer a tent or even a building, it is His people (see Acts 17:24; 1 Cor. 3:16; 6:19; I Pet. 2:5).

When God's people *find their place* in the makeup of His house, God's glory shall be evident! Finding our place is a work of the Holy

Spirit within each believer. It is confirmed by the leadership of the local church and by the anointing for service.

We are "living stones" of all different shapes and size that God puts together to build a spiritual house (I Pet. 2:5). Each individual is personally designed by God Himself. A calling, and the gifts to fulfill that calling, were deposited in each of us from our mother's womb (see Jer. 1:5; Gal. 1:15). Allowing the Holy Spirit to separate us to that calling under the authority of a local church is that which makes us a "Glorious Church" (Eph. 5:27).

To properly understand the function church leadership, it is imperative to understand the offices and functions of the five-fold ministry. The church is to be governed by the five-fold ministry, namely the pastor in regards to the local level.

In the Book of Acts, the government of the church was in the hands of the five-fold ministry, where God placed it. The early church had the pattern, therefore, the glory. The reason many churches today don't have the glory of God in them is that they're not under the government of God-appointed, five-fold ministries – the first foundational stone of divine order (see Eph. 2:20-22).

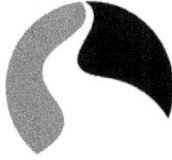

Five-Fold Ministry

The ministry gifts that God has given to the church are listed in Ephesians chapter four:

Ephesians 4:11-14

11 And He Himself gave some to be apostles, some prophets, some evangelists, and some pastors and teachers,

12 for the equipping of the saints for the work of ministry, for the edifying of the body of Christ,

13 till we all come to the unity of the faith and of the knowledge of the Son of God, to a perfect man, to the measure of the stature of the fullness of Christ;

14 that we should no longer be children, tossed to and fro and carried about with every wind of doctrine, by the trickery of men, in the cunning craftiness of deceitful plotting

For the body of Christ to reach its full potential, it is important to understand and receive the five-fold ministries and their gifts. The following are brief descriptions of the apostle, prophet, evangelist, pastor, and teacher:

Apostles: Literally "sent ones." There are three levels of apostles:

1. The "Sent One" from the Father: Jesus, the One and Only Apostle of the Father (see John 17:18a; Heb. 3:1).

2. The "sent ones" from the Son: The Twelve. The twelve are in a class to themselves. There will never be another foundational (Eph. 2:20) apostle (See Rev. 21:14; John 17:18b).

3. The "sent ones" from the Holy Spirit: Paul and the other apostles called after Christ's ascension. This would include modern day apostles. These are termed "Body-building" apostles, rather than foundational. Paul was the exception, being a foundational, Scripture-writing apostle. According to Scriptural exactness, the twelve do not qualify as an Ephesian 4:11 apostle; these are post-ascension apostles; the twelve were pre-ascension apostles (See Acts 13:2-4; Eph. 4:8, 11).

Apostles are primarily involved in the pioneering and establishing of local churches. Paul said in Romans 15:20: "And so I have made it my aim to preach the gospel not where Christ was named lest I should build on another man's foundation."

Apostles are spiritual fathers to other ministries. There is such a need for spiritual fathers and mentors in the Body of Christ. Every Timothy reeds a Paul to take him under his wing and develop him. Paul wrote to the Corinthians: "For though you might have ten thousand instructors in Christ, yet you do not have many fathers; for in Christ Jesus I have begotten you through the gospel" (I Cor. 4:15).

Signs and wonders will accompany the apostle. Paul said in 2 Corinthians 12:12: "Truly the signs of an apostle were accomplished among you with all perseverance, in signs and wonders and mighty deeds." Heaven's validation of the apostolic gift is the miraculous in operation. Not that miracles occur only through apostles. But any claim to apostleship must be accompanied by a regular occurrence of signs and wonders.

An apostle's ministry will include discipline and correction. Apostles are especially concerned with areas of doctrine. When a pastor or church gets into error, the apostolic gift is greatly needed.

Apostles are involved in the training and ordination of ministries. This can be seen in Paul's continual references to imparting to those under him such as Timothy and Titus. The training of ministries is the heartbeat of an apostle's ministry.

Prophets: There are three major realms of prophecy:

1. Prophecy of Scripture (1 Pet. 1:20-21). This level of prophecy is complete. All other prophecy must be judged by the Prophecy of Scripture.
2. The Office of the Prophet (I Cor. 12:28; Eph. 4:11). This is someone who operates in the ministry gift of the prophet.
3. The Gift of Prophecy (I Cor. 12:10; 14:1, 3, 6). All believers are open to this manifestation of the Spirit. The gift must be operated within the guidelines of Scripture (see I Cor. 14).

A prophet is used to give direction to the church. This is not a controlling directive, but a confirming one. At times, prophets will give direction to individuals, especially those in authority. The prophet Agabus is recorded as prophesying to both the corporate church and individuals:

- The church, Acts 11:27-29

- An individual (Paul), Acts 21:10-11.

A prophet's ministry involves revelation, confirmation and warning. The prophet's ministry is especially valuable in identifying and confirming ministry gifts within a presbytery setting (see Acts 13:1-3; I Tim. 4:14).

A prophet will operate in the gift of prophecy, as well as the word of knowledge, word of wisdom, and discerning of spirits. Simply operating in the gift of prophecy does not make one a prophet.

A genuine prophet's words will come to pass. There are many self-proclaimed prophets in the land who do not wish their words to be judged for accuracy. However, the Bible mandate is: "Let two or three prophets speak and let the others judge" (I Cor. 14:29). A prophet who will not submit to authority and be accountable for his words is not to be heeded (see Deuteronomy 18:22).

Evangelists: Gather in the lost. Theirs is an emphasis of preaching the gospel to sinners.

There will be a certain "fire" to an evangelist's preaching. It could be termed as "revival-type preaching." The word "gospel" means "Good News!" Therefore, an evangelist will carry a message that is narrower in scope than the other five-fold ministries. An evangelist is not called to expound doctrine and theology. Many have been side-tracked by getting out of their anointing.

Evangelists are an equipping ministry, like all of the five-fold gifts. They are given to train believers how to win souls. Too much responsibility is given to the evangelist to win the world by themselves. Their job is to train us all to fulfill the great commission (Matt. 28:19-20; Mark 16:15-20).

Philip is the only one who is named an evangelist in the entire New Testament (Acts 21:8). Philip began as a deacon and God promoted him. He went to Samaria and held public meetings in which multitudes were saved. God worked miracles through Philip that got the people's attention:

> **Acts 8:6**
> **The multitudes with one accord heeded the things spoken by Philip, hearing and seeing the miracles which he did.**

A true evangelist will have the operation of miracles in his ministry. Signs still point men to Jesus!

In the middle of this revival, Philip obeyed the Lord and went to the desert to win one man to the Lord (Acts 8:26-39). True evangelists have a passion to win souls, both publicly and one at a time.

This ministry is instrumental to the growth of local churches. An evangelist should work in coordination with the local churches in any designated field. Christ's command is not only to convert sinners, but to disciple them. An evangelist should also have a home local church that he is submitted to and from which he works.

Pastors: Literally "shepherds." Pastors tend the flock of God, taking direct oversight.

> **I Peter 5:2-3 exhorts pastors: Shepherd the flock of God which is among you, serving as overseers, not by constraint but willingly, not for dishonest gain but eagerly; nor as being**

lords over those entrusted to you, but being examples to the flock.

Pastoring is a ministry of feeding, leading and guarding the sheep. The authority to lead is predicated by the ability to feed. Having a good heart does not qualify one to be a pastor, nor does an educated mind. The ability to feed the sheep comes from the calling and anointing of God. While the other four gifts may itinerate, the pastor's primary responsibility is the local church. Thus we have the heavy emphasis that is placed on this office in respect to the local church. Pastors are the primary care givers to the local congregation.

Though pastors are in the primary leadership position in the local church, they cannot do their job without the other four ministries. A congregation needs to be influenced by all five of the ministry gifts to be brought to maturity (see Ephesians. 4:11-13).

Teachers: Ground God's people in the Word of God.

These are not Sunday school teachers, but anointed ministers that bring clarity and understanding to the Word of God. They are avid students of the Word themselves, studying to show themselves approved unto God (2 Tim. 2:15). Someone who has no desire to study is definitely not called to be a teacher.

A teacher must guard against becoming just another "echo." The teachers in Christ's day were just echoes of the rabbis. God wants a teacher to be a voice not an echo! When Christ the Pattern Teacher taught, people were astonished at His anointing: "And so it was, when Jesus had ended these sayings, that the people were astonished at His teaching, for He taught them as one having authority, and not as the scribes" (Matt. 7:28-29).

14

Teachers desire to see others come up to their level of understanding and even surpass them. A teacher is not a lecturer that impresses everyone with his knowledge. If no one is learning then no one is teaching! To preach is to proclaim; to teach is to explain.

A teacher should be a sound theologian, well-rounded, not just teaching one subject or doctrine: A teacher should also be a sound hermeneutician, that is, be able to "rightly divide the Word of Truth" (2 Tim 2:15b). Some who call themselves teachers have never developed these skills. The Body should not have to suffer in doctrine just to have the Spirit! Qualified teachers know how to expound the whole truth in a rightly divided manner in the power of the Spirit.

Multiple Offices

These five offices serve the Body of Chris as equipping ministries. Ephesians 4:11 says that only "some" are called to these equipping ministries. It is also stated that only God can do the calling: "And He gave..." In the original Greek this is in the intensive form, literally saying, "He, Himself, and no other gave."

It is possible for a person to be called to more than one office at a time, in 1 Timothy 2:7 Paul refers to himself as an apostle and a teacher. It is also possible to "graduate" to a higher office than previously used in. This is usually the case with the office of apostle. Paul was also called a prophet and a teacher before his apostolic setting apart:

> **Acts 13:1-4a**
> **1 Now there were in the church that was at Antioch certain prophets and teachers; as Barnabas, and Simeon that was**

called Niger, and Lucius of Cyrene, and Manaen, which had been brought up with Herod the tetrarch, and Saul.

2 As they ministered to the Lord, and fasted, the Holy Ghost said, Separate me Barnabas and Saul for the work whereunto I have called them.

3 And when they had fasted and prayed, and laid their hands on them, they sent them away.

4 So they, being sent forth by the Holy Ghost...

Notice that Paul had been standing in the office of prophet and teacher. At this point Paul had been saved for approximately ten years. When the Holy Ghost spoke, He spoke in terms of separation to a calling that Barnabas and Paul (Saul) had not previously stood in. From that point forth it was "Paul the apostle."

The Work of the Ministry

As previously stated, all of the five-fold offices are equipping ministries. Let us be reminded of the goals of the five-fold ministry, as listed in Ephesians 4:12-16:

12 For the perfecting of the saints, for the work of the ministry, for the edifying of the body of Christ:

13 Till we all come in the unity of the faith, and of the knowledge of the Son of God, unto a perfect man, unto the measure of the stature of the fullness of Christ:

14 That we henceforth be no more children, tossed to and fro, and carried about with every wind of doctrine, by the sleight of men, and cunning craftiness, whereby they lie in wait to deceive;

15 But speaking the truth in love, may grow up into him in all things, which is the head, even Christ:

16 from whom the whole body, joined and knit together by what every joint supplies, according to the effective working

by which every part does its share, causes growth of the body for the edifying of itself in love.

The Body of Christ is to do the work of the ministry. The ministry of the believer and the priesthood of the believer is never minimized or diminished by the five-fold ministry. The five-fold ministries serve to maximize the ministry and priesthood of every believer. If any of the five-fold ministries is neglected then the Body becomes less effective in essential areas listed in Ephesians 4:12-16, such as:

- The work of the ministry
- Edification
- Unity
- Knowledge
- Maturity
- Doctrine
- Truth
- Love
- The working of every part.

Governing Offices

Out of these five offices, three of them are primarily involved in governing, on the basis of their function and place of operation. They are the apostle, the prophet, and the pastor.

- **Apostle:** The apostle oversees many churches, being a spiritual father, giving correction when needed.

- **Prophet:** The prophet gives insight and confirmation into the operation of local churches. If the leadership is off course, he brings rebuke and/or adjustment.

- o Note: the apostle and prophet's ministry is wider in scope than one local church. They are not involved in the everyday affairs of local church life.

- **Pastor:** The role of the pastor is involved in the everyday affairs of the local church. Therefore, the office of the pastor is the primary governing ministry of the local church. He does not operate independently of the apostle and prophet, or for that matter the evangelist and teacher. The pastor works in cooperation with the other ministry gifts. Ideally, each pastor should be submitted to an apostle.

In fact, may who are called "pastor" are standing in the office of multiple gifts such as apostle, prophet, teacher. However, due to failure to understand the purpose and nature of these gifts, the title of pastor is used to encompass everything. For that matter, none of the five gifts are *titles* but rather job descriptions – functions. Respect cannot be demanded on the basis of a title. Title power will not set anyone free, only the power of the Holy Spirit.

A local church should have the entire five-fold ministry in function. Some gifts may be local – within the church body, while others may be itinerant. The itinerant ministries, though not full-time within the church body, will have a voice into the church, as designated by God.

Pastoral Church Government

The above description has become commonly known as "Pastoral Church Government." When operated with proper checks and balances, this is proper order. Some may disagree and say that the church should be governed by a group of ministers/elders who are equal in authority. While there should be a ministry team and a group of elders in every church, there has to be one head for proper order. In other words, **there should be plurality of leadership, but there cannot be plurality of headship**.

In the New Testament there are three analogies given to the local church:

1. The Universal Church
2. The human body
3. The marriage relationship

All three of these have only one head! It is clear that the local church should have one head. There should be government over the head (e.g., church fellowship, ordaining organization, apostolic authority), and government under the head (e.g., associate pastors, elders, deacons). However, the ones *over* him and the ones *under* him cannot be the same people.

When God was selecting Moses' successor, listen to what Moses said to God:

Numbers 27:16-17

16 Let the LORD, the God of the spirits of all flesh set a man over the congregation,

17 who may go out before them and go in before them who may lead them out and bring them in, that the congregation of the LORD may not be like sheep which have no shepherd [pastor].

There must be a "Set Man" over the congregation. Headship is not dictatorship. Headship is for the establishment of order. There is even order in the Godhead, 1 Corinthians 11:3 says, "The Head of Christ is God." Christ is equal in terms of deity, but He is submitted to the Father in terms of order. The set man, or the lead pastor, is not better than the other ministries in the church, but in terms of order, God has placed him at the head.

God sets the members in the Body, every one of them, as it pleases Him (1 Cor. 12:18). It is not man's choice who should be in charge. Man-appointed leadership has bankrupted the church of the power of God for too long.

Jesus addressed the seven churches of the Roman province of Asia in the book of Revelation through the letters of the Apostle John. Each letter to the seven churches was addressed to "the angel" of each respective church. We know that heavenly angels weren't governing those churches. The word "angel" (angelos) literally means "messenger." Jesus was speaking to the messenger of each church. He said *the messenger*, singular not plural. So while there is plurality of leadership, there is not plurality of headship. As one preacher said, "Anything with more than one head is a monster."

There was plurality of leadership at the church in Jerusalem, but James was the head. This is clear from Acts chapter 15. We will discuss the role of James further, later in the module.

Two Levels of Elders

In understanding the role of elders, it is important to know that there are two levels of elders:

1. **Five-fold Elders**
2. **Supportive Elders**

All five-fold ministers are elders themselves. Consider the following Scriptures:

- 1 Peter 5:1 The elders who are among you I exhort, I [Peter] who am a fellow elder.
- Both the 2nd and 3rd epistles of the Apostle John begin with "The Elder to..."

All of the five-fold ministry offices are elders. These are the ruling elders. They are called to govern the church of the living God. It should be noted that all that give themselves the title of "pastor" are not called by God. But those that are, are hand-picked and groomed by the Holy Spirit for the task.

God said in Jeremiah 3:15: I will give you pastors according to My heart.

God's pastors are not perfect. However, if God looked beyond their faults to give them the gift and the office, then God's people must look beyond their faults and submit to them.

This distinction and separation in elders can be clearly seen in 1 Timothy 5:17:

> **Let the elders who rule well be counted worthy of double honor, especially those who labor in the Word and doctrine.**

The elders *who rule* are the ones who labor in the ministry of the Word. Not all do this, as is indicated by the word "especially" concerning those who do. The term "double honor" is referring to financial provision. Five-fold elders should be supported by the church. The government of the church should be in the hands of those who are directing its affairs on a full-time basis, not in the hands of businessmen who are not called into the five-fold ministry. They have their businesses to run; God has not chosen to qualify them to run the church also. They have their expertise to offer in a supportive role, but those outside of the five-fold calling do not govern the church, except in the supportive role.

When Paul begins to list the qualifications of an elder in 1 Timothy chapter three, he starts off by saying: "This is a faithful saying: If a man desires the position of a bishop [elder], he desires a good work" (3:1). This again shows the distinction and separation of elders, for one cannot enter a five-fold ministry because he *desires* to, he must be called by God. However, a person can desire to become a supportive elder and enter into that role. It should also be noted that God may use a person in a supportive role before He separates him to a five-fold one. Philip was a deacon before he was an evangelist. The process is good hands-on training.

The first mention of appointing elders in the New Testament is found in Acts 14:23: "They [Paul and Barnabas] appointed elders in every church" Please note two things from this first mention:

1. These elders were man-appointed; their call did not come directly through God, as with five-fold ministries.
2. The ones who appoint you are over you in authority. God Himself appoints five-fold ministries, and He is over them.

Traditional Forms of Church Government

A Three-Fold Cord

There are three traditional forms of church government. There are positives and negatives found in each. Imposing one of them without regard to the others will result in imbalance and injury to God's purposes and His people.

The three types of church government are:

1. **Episcopal** (derived from Greek word for "bishop" or "overseer"): A presiding elder, having been appointed by an overseeing bishop, rules the church. Basically it is a one-man form of government on a local level.

2. **Presbyterial** (derived from the Greek word for "elder"): A plurality of elders rule the church with equal power. The appointment of which comes from the congregation.

3. **Congregational**: A democratic form of government that gives the people the right to hire and fire the pastor, and direct the affairs of the church by voting. It is a committee oriented government.

These forms of government obviously entail much more detail, but this is the basic premise of each. As stated, there are positives and negatives in each of the three traditional forms of church government. Below, I have listed what I see as the major strengths and weaknesses of each system:

Episcopal
- Strengths: Biblical in its one head (lead pastor) form of government; limits authority to those who are genuinely called of God.
- Weaknesses: Potential danger if the one head is of a domineering, Diotrephes-type spirit (see III John 9-10); No checks and balances.

Presbyterial
- Strengths: Multiple elders provide checks and balances against dictatorship; spreads out the spiritual load instead of it being on one man.
- Weaknesses: Gives no one the mantle of leadership as head, under Christ. Often leaves a church without a God-given vision, as vision primarily comes to individuals (see Acts 26:19).

Congregational
- Strengths: Actively involves the congregation in church matters; gives people a feel of ownership, thus are willing to sacrifice.
- Weaknesses: The Biblical pattern is a Theocracy (God-ruled), not Democracy (people-ruled); strips God-appointed leaders of their authority; "Laodicea" literally means "people-ruled" (see Rev. 3:14-17).

Ecclesiastes 4:12 says: "A threefold cord is not quickly broken." The early church operated a government that was comprised of the strengths of each of the three traditional forms of church government. The history of the Church shows repeatedly that man takes a portion of divine truth and tries to make it a whole. That is why there are so many denominations with different points of emphasis. Restoration involves taking the good out of the present and eliminating the bad. Even an old cow is smart enough to eat the hay and spit out the sticks.

In the book of Acts we can see the early church operating in the strengths of all three systems. One place that they can all be found together is at the first Church council in Acts chapter 15. The apostles and elders were meeting to discuss the problems that arose with the great influx of Gentile believers. Should circumcision be done away with and so forth? The student should read verses 1-22 for a complete understanding. For the purpose of the subject at hand I only quote that which pertains to each of the three forms of government.

- **Presbyterial**: "So the apostles and elders came to consider this matter" (v. 6).
- **Episcopal**: "Therefore I [James] judge that we should not trouble those from among the Gentiles who are turning to God" (v. 19).
- **Congregational**: "Then it pleased the apostles and elders with the whole church" (v. 22).

The decision by James, as the Lead pastor at the Church of Jerusalem, was made only after listening to the counsel of the apostles and elders. As the head of the local church at Jerusalem, James was responsible for making the final decision. However, he exercised much wisdom by consulting with those of spiritual maturity and experience. The congregation had complete confidence in their God-appointed leaders. The decision from James pleased not only the apostles and elders, but the entire congregation.

James, as the Lead pastor, was making himself accountable for his decisions. He was not a dictator that ruled independently of the counsel of the elders or the well-being of the congregation.

Who is Over the Pastors?

Like James, today's pastors need a system of checks and balances to make them accountable. God needs men and women of integrity. Those who are God-appointed welcome the oversight and counsel of spiritual fathers. We should learn from the mistakes of recent ministries that have fallen. Let us not forget to "consider ourselves lest we also be tempted" (Gal. 6:1).

Five-fold ministers should govern themselves through a presbytery, a group of five-fold elders in covenant agreement. Fellow ministers that have covenanted together to build up the Body of Christ, and help one another fulfill their callings is a divine pattern of ministry and covering. Everyone needs a covering, especially those on the front lines. May the Lord give us more spiritual fathers and men and women with the loyal hearts of a Jonathan (see 1 Samuel 18).

The ordaining organization of a pastor should serve as an overseeing body. Denominations have built-in oversight in their government, but independent works often lack a true covering. Sadly many ordaining organizations have little or nothing to do with their ministers. Just an annual renewal fee keeps them current as an affiliated minister.

God has divine connections for His servants. Without such, a spirit of isolation will try to creep in to the pastor's heart. Independence should not mean isolation! The ordaining organization should serve as a point of oversight, and, if need be, correction. But if that isn't the case, a minister should seek out some type of minister's fellowship in which to affiliate.

Submission to an apostolic authority is also recommended. Only those submitted authority can in authority. Pastors must be willing to submit to people over them in the Lord, and to one another (1 Pet. 5:5).

I was ordained by Lester Sumrall in 1990 and have maintained a close relationship with that ministry. It has been a source of direction for me and God has used that ministry countless times to speak into my life. Dr. Sumrall was a true apostle according to Scripture and his sons continue to carry that mantle.

The purpose in accountability is not to bring people into denominational bondage (it's possible to be in a denomination without being in bondage). The purpose is to love one another, network our ministries, give prayerful counsel, and protect the flock. The objective is not to control! The spirit of competition must be avoided, because where there is competition, control follows close behind. This is what has happened in many denominations.

One final note about apostolic covering over pastors and churches: the apostolic covering does not dictate over the pastor or the church. A review of the small epistle of Philemon reveals how an apostle provides guidance. Paul was sending back Onesimus to Philemon and the church in his house. Instead of telling Philemon what he was *going to do*, he instead sought his consent and cooperation.

> **Philemon 1:14**
> **But without your consent I wanted to do nothing, that your good deed might not be by compulsion, as it were, but voluntary.**

The members of the congregation should have full knowledge of the relationships of their pastors with the overseeing fellowship. In doing so, an example of submission is set for them to follow towards their pastors. As well, there should be some policy in place where the people under a leader can have him removed if he gets into error. Supportive elders are in place to provide this type of protection. I have drawn up a pastoral covenant agreement that monitors the office of the pastor in regards to three areas of concern:

1. Doctrinal Error
2. Moral Failure
3. Financial Mishandling.

Procedures are given in that covenant agreement for dealing with a pastor who has fallen prey to the above problems. The days have come where the truly called and anointed of God want accountability in their ministries. If we do not judge ourselves, we will be judged by the Lord (1 Cor. 11:31-32).

Pastors, elders, deacons, and the entire congregation, along with the apostles, prophets, evangelists, and teachers must work together, each finding their place in the house of God. When that divine pattern is reached, we should expect the glory to fill the house!

Consider what the Apostle Paul wrote in 1 Timothy 3:15:

I write so that you may know how you ought to conduct yourself in the house of God which is the church of the living God, the pillar and ground of truth.

When Leaders Fall Into Sin

What happens when a leader falls into sin? Should there be immediate restoration? Should there be complete removal? Does the Bible tell us how the church should respond? Much debate has centered on these and other questions. The solution of some has been to just ignore the problem and hope it goes away on its own. It doesn't.

The Bible specifically tells us how to respond to a leader that falls into sin. The passage is found in 1 Timothy 5:19-22. After reading it we will dissect the different steps of the process.

> **1Timothy 5:19-22**
> **19 Do not receive an accusation against an elder except from two or three witnesses.**
> **20 Those who are sinning rebuke in the presence of all, that the rest also may fear.**
> **21 I charge you before God and the Lord Jesus Christ and the elect angels that you observe these things without prejudice, doing nothing with partiality.**
> **22 Do not lay hands on anyone hastily, nor share in other people's sins.**

Step #1: (v. 19) Due to the honor of the position, a leader must not be accused without two or three reliable witnesses. The church is told to not receive any accusations which are unconfirmed. This is difficult for some, as many want to believe the worst about a leader on the basis of hearsay.

Upon the evidence of two or three reliable witnesses, a leader is to be confronted about his sin. He should be given the facts of the witnesses and given an opportunity to either confirm or deny them. When it becomes established that the elder has fallen into sin, the church leadership should proceed with step #2.

Step #2: (v. 20) The sinning leader should be publicly rebuked. There are certain situations where this would not apply. However, we must not change the instructions of the Holy Word of God! The purpose of this rebuke is not to humiliate the offender but to cause the congregation to fear God. A little leaven leavens the whole lump. When sin is tolerated among the leadership, it will run rampant in the congregation.

What type of sin would require this extreme measure? The list in 1 Corinthians 5:11 and 6:9-10 serves well:

    a. Fornicator
    b. Covetous man
    c. Idolater
    d. Reviler
    e. Drunkard
    f. Extortioner
    g. Adulterer
    h. Homosexual
    i. Sodomite
    j. Thief

These types of offenders have no place in the Kingdom of God (I Cor. 6:9-10). The Church is forbidden to fellowship with them (I Cor. 5:11). Certainly they have no place in leadership.

Step #3: (v. 21) These instructions are to be followed without prejudice and partiality. Regardless of how well-liked an individual is, there can be no partiality in administering divine correction.

Step #4: Verse 22 says: "Do not lay hands on anyone hastily." This is making reference to the appointment of leaders. Keeping with the context of the passage, it refers to the reinstatement of leaders. The counterpoint of this admonition is: "Nor share in other people's sins" (v. 22b). By laying hands on an offending leader too hastily to reinstate him, the leadership team is sharing in the sin of the former leader.

If reinstatement is *not* to be done hastily, the conclusion is that it is to be done patiently and progressively. Some believe that it should not be done at all, but this isn't what Paul is saying. There are certain instances of failure where restoration to leadership is not capable. However, this does not preclude one from restoration to God and the family of God.

In most cases the patient and progressive route is available. This would be considered a probationary period. How long should this be? It is dependent on the individual progress of the person, as well as the level of failure from which one is overcoming. The family of the leader being restored is also of primary consideration. Rushing back into ministry can result in further damage.

Obviously, there can be other types of personal failures that do not require such a lengthy process. Further, the above mentioned timeframe should not be approached in a legalistic way; there will always be exceptions. On the flip side, there are some who will not respond to correction whether it's two years or twenty years. The bottom line is that Biblical restoration can be successfully completed.

The process may seem slow, but it is well worth the effort and time spent.

Study Questions, Part 1

1. What caused judgment to fall when David first tried to bring the Ark to Zion?

_____

_____

_____

_____

2. Define the term "Divine Order."

_____

_____

_____

_____

3. How is each believer's "place" confirmed within a local body?

_____

_____

_____

_____

4. Should the Church be governed by elders and deacons, or the five-fold ministry? Why?

_____

_____

_____

_____

5. What is the first foundational stone of divine order? What Scripture shows this?

_____

_____

_____

6. Give a brief definition of each of the five ministry gifts.

1. _____

2. _____

3. _____

4. _____

5. _____

7. What are the three levels of apostles?

1. _____

2. _____

3. _____

8. What are the three major realms of prophecy?

1. _____

2. _____

3. _____

9. Who is the only evangelist named in the New Testament?

_____

10. Which ministry gift is the primary caregiver to the local church?

_____

11. What is the difference between preaching and teaching?
Preaching:

_____

Teaching:

_____

12. Why is the office of pastor the primary governing ministry of the local church?

_____

_____

_____

_____

13. There should be plurality of _____, but there cannot be plurality of _____.

14. In the New Testament there are three analogies given to the local church; what are they?

1. _____

2. _____

3. _____

15. What were the "Angels" of the seven churches of Asia Minor?

_____

16. What are the two levels of elders in the New Testament? What scripture shows this distinction?

_____

_____

_____

17. Which of the two levels of elders are ruling elders?

_____

18. Why shouldn't businessmen be the ones running the church?

_____

_____

19. What are the three traditional forms of church government? What is one strength and weakness of each?

1.

_____

_____

2.

_____

_____

3.

_____

_____

20. Where in the New Testament can all three forms of government be seen at work simultaneously?

_____

_____

21. Who was the Senior Pastor at Jerusalem? How did he show much wisdom?

_____

_____

22. What is a presbytery and how does it function?

_____

_____

_____

_____

23. Only those _____ to authority can be in _____.

24. Name some of the purposes of accountability.

_____

_____

_____

_____

25. What three areas of concern are covered in the "Pastoral Contract"?

1.

_____

_____

2.

_____

_____

3.

_____

_____

Section Two: Delegation & The Appointment of Elders

Delegated Authority and Submission

Romans 13:1-2 Let every soul be subject to the governing authorities. For there is no authority except from God, and the authorities that exist are appointed by God. Therefore whoever resists the authority resists the ordinance of God, and those who resist will bring judgment on themselves.

Heaven is God's throne and the earth is His footstool, everything God does is ruled in order. Authorities exist because God instituted them; they are the "ordinance of God." Authorities exist in spiritual, domestic and civil realms, and every other facet of society. To rebel against authority is to rebel against God!

God's Church is established upon the authority of its Head – the Lord Jesus Christ. However, God has ordained delegated authority under Christ to carry out His purposes in the Church. These authorities are primarily the five-fold ministries He has set in the Church (1 Cor. 12:18). Beyond that, on a local level, we see that there is a chain of command instituted by God Himself.

Scripture teaches us that each local church is to be autonomous, that is, self-governing. Within that self-government there are several authorities which are delegated by God. The order of delegated authority within a given local church would be as follows:

1. **Jesus Christ, the Head of the Church**; both universal and local. Unless Christ is the Head, all those after Him are laboring in vain (Ps. 127:1). The human body cannot function properly and in coordination without the direct signals of the head. Even so, the Body of Christ cannot properly function without the direct involvement and guidance of its Head, Jesus Christ.

2. **The Lead Pastor** is essentially the "set man" over the congregation (Num. 27:16). The lead pastor is the primary under-shepherd, under Christ. The lead pastor is responsible for the vision and the implementation of that vision, which entails the facilitation of key roles to those under him. He is an overseer of the overseers. The final decisions are his responsibility (Acts 15:19).

3. **The Pastoral Staff:** As a church grows this necessitates the need for more pastoral care. A pastoral staff would consist of associates and assistants. Youth pastors and music ministers may also fall into this category, if so designated by the lead pastor. The pastoral staff is directly submitted to the lead pastor.
   The primary role of the pastoral staff is not preaching from the pulpit, though it does not exclude it, but pastoral care to the flock – personal ministry. The congregation and elders should show respect and submission to the pastoral staff for they are the representatives of the lead pastor.

4. **The Elders:** Supportive elders are not five-fold in function or authority, but a ministry of helps. They undergird and support the pastors. They are burden-bearers. Supportive elders provide pastoral care to the flock by way of prayer, counseling and personal ministry.

The authority of a supportive elder is conditional upon the job description of each elder. If an elder is in charge of the follow-up ministry, then that elder is in authority over the follow-up. However, that same elder is not in authority over the Sunday school ministry. By no means is this an unconditional authority. Elders must be submitted to the entire pastoral staff and ultimately to the lead pastor. Major decisions are not to be made without consulting those in authority.

5. **The Deacons:** Although not a governmental ministry by definition, a deacon is still in a leadership role. A deacon should be a role model servant. Deacons oversee the physical aspects of church life, and are often called upon to meet spiritual needs by the congregation (e.g., Philip, Stephen). Deacons are under the direct supervision of the elders and are ultimately accountable to the lead pastor.

Submission to those over you in the Lord is a key factor in one's ultimate success or failure in the things of God. One cannot be in authority who has not submitted to authority.

Hebrews 13:17 Obey those who rule over you, and be submissive, for they watch out for your souls, as those who must give account. Let them do so with joy and not with grief, for that would be unprofitable for you.

I have the following written in the back of my study Bible:

Four types of people present opposition to your assignment, vision and ministry:

1. Those who don't receive it
2. Those who don't respect it

3. Those who don't protect it
4. Those who don't believe that you can achieve it

When the lead pastor selects those who will help serve the flock in official roles, careful consideration should be given to *not* select someone who meets any of the above descriptions.

When Jesus selected the 12, He spent all night with the Father in prayer:

> **Luke 6**
> **12 Now it came to pass in those days that He went out to the mountain to pray, and continued all night in prayer to God.**
> **13 And when it was day, He called His disciples to Himself; and from them He chose twelve whom He also named apostles**

There were many disciples following Jesus at that point. Jesus didn't just pick 12 random men. Some track records had been established.

Jesus spent all night with God in prayer and carefully selected the 12 based on the Father's will. A pastor cannot just pick men based on the outward appearance or someone's success in the business arena. Those appointed to leadership in the church must be prayerfully and carefully chosen.

Board of Directors

Most autonomous churches are non-profit corporations. The government recognizes this as 501(c)3 status. The board of directors of a corporation governs the business affairs of that organization. There are several privileges attained by incorporating including:

a. Tax-exempt status.
b. Protection for individual members against lawsuits (though the corporation itself may be sued).
c. Individual members are also shielded from personal liability for the debts of the corporation.

Certain requirements must be met before a church can incorporate. The government is imposing itself more and more upon the affairs of the Church. The 501(c)3 status is not given out as readily as in the past. The financial mishandlings of some big ministries have largely contributed to this. A non-profit corporation cannot be established for the business of making a profit. This is not to say that its officers cannot have a salary, but it must be considered reasonable and not excessive.

Requirements for non-profit incorporation include:

- Preparing articles of incorporation: pertinent information about the organization.

- Having a Constitution and Bylaws: the rules of internal government.
- Having a minimum of three board members and a maximum of nine. President, Vice-President, Secretary and Treasurer are mandatory. The same person may hold two or more offices (other than president and secretary).
- Maintaining records: financial records and minutes of board meetings.
- Conducting an annual business meeting.

The president should be the lead pastor. The other positions should be filled by people of integrity and spiritual maturity, chosen from among the pastoral staff and elders. Additional board members may be termed advisors. An advisor may be selected from outside the immediate body. If the pastor has a spiritual father or an apostle that he is submitted to, this person would serve well as an advisor.

Although an elder may be selected to be on the board of directors, the board is separate from the elder's ministry. The two functions are not to be confused. Being an elder does not entitle one to make business decisions for the church. This is the function of the board of directors.

The Jerusalem Model

Acts chapter 15 records the first general council of the New Testament Church. As previously mentioned, dissention had entered the Church over the influx of Gentile believers. Paul was the apostle to the Gentiles and he had been having a mighty move of God. Gentiles were receiving the gospel far more readily than the Jews. The dispute was over the Law of Moses, especially circumcision. Should the Gentile believers be circumcised and obey the Mosaic Law?

The following is an excerpt from that meeting:

> **Acts 15:**
> **2 Therefore when Paul and Barnabas had no small dissension and dispute with them, they determined that Paul and Barnabas and certain others of them should go up to Jerusalem, to the apostles and elders, about this question.**
> **6 So the apostles and elders, came together to consider this matter.**
> **7 And when there had been much dispute, Peter rose up and said to them: "Men and brethren, you know that a good while ago God chose among us, that by my mouth the Gentiles should hear the word of the gospel and believe."**

12 Then all the multitude kept silent and listened to Barnabas and Paul declaring how many miracles and wonders God had worked through them among the Gentiles.

13 And after they had become silent James answered saying, "Men and brethren, listen to me…

19 Therefore I judge that we should not trouble those from among the Gentiles who are turning to God"…

22 Then it pleased the apostles and elders, with the whole church

There was a coming together of the apostles and elders over this matter. No one person was in a position to hand down a decision without such a meeting. Paul and Barnabas represented the interests of the Gentiles. Peter also spoke up for the Gentile believers. Remember it was Peter that first brought the gospel to a Gentile household (Acts 10).

There was a chain of command or authority at the Church of Jerusalem. It was not a dictatorship but James, the half-brother of the Lord, was the head, or the lead pastor at Jerusalem. After much discussion and prayer James arose and gave his decision (v. 19). Wait a minute, didn't they take a vote? No! Remember, the House of the Lord is not governed by a democracy (people-ruled), but a theocracy (God-ruled). God rules through delegated authority. James was the man that God hand-picked to be in charge of the Jerusalem church. The final decision was his.

The rest of the apostles and elders, along with the congregation, submitted to the judgment of James (v. 22). A wise leader will listen to those God has placed around him. He will also listen to the Holy Spirit, and be bold enough to make a decision. A lead pastor cannot be double-minded, back and forth. And, if so required by the Holy Spirit, he must be able to rise up against the tide of popular opinion and take a stand. At that point the elders should stand with their leadership (unless morally, doctrinally, or ethically in error) and give their full support. A divided spirit cannot be allowed!

Moses' System of Delegation

Exodus 18:21 Moreover you shall select from all the people able men, such as fear God, men of truth, hating covetousness: and place such over them to be rulers of thousands, rulers of hundreds, rulers of fifties, and rulers of tens.

The delegation of authority by Moses was based upon each individual elder's ability. Some were given more responsibility than others. Yet each had their own segment of the congregation that they were responsible for. They were to deal with and resolve the small matters and bring the great matters to Moses.

Some church government experts think that a local church needs a supportive elder per every ten families. The average family equals out to 2.5 people; this means that for every 25 people in the congregation an elder is needed. A church of 100 would need four elders.

Number of Members	Elders Needed
100	4
200	8
300	12
500	20
1000	40

Of course it doesn't always work out this way, for many reasons. But it is a good guideline to grow by. It has also been said that a pastor can only truly pastor about 200 people. At that point, major changes have to be made to accommodate further growth. Delegation of authority and facilitation of ministry have to be accepted by the congregation to move beyond that barrier. If it has not been a practice up to this point, rough sailing lies ahead. Jesus put the principle of delegation and facilitation into practice with twelve. Start when you're small!

If an elder is assigned to ten families, what does this entail? The following is a list of some of the responsibilities involved:

- Making sure each family is in attendance at the worship services, and if not, finding out why.
- Being available for personal ministry through the week and before and after services.
- Helping to resolve any conflicts or division that occurs with those families and someone else in the church. Enforcing Matthew 18:15-17.
- Representing the pastors in a positive light at all times.
- Regularly calling and/or visiting the ten families of one's responsibility.
- The members of the congregation are to call their assigned elder if personal ministry or prayer is needed (James 5:14).

The pastors should give great prayer and attention to the selection of members under a particular elder's care. If problems arise within the relationship, the pastors should step in and resolve it. At times it is best to reassign the member to another elder (after strife has been resolved).

Under this system of delegation an elder has authority within the boundaries of his assignment. At all times, an elder is an extension of the pastoral office. The authority of the elder goes only as far as his submission to the pastor extends it. To avoid a sectarian spirit from developing it may be necessary to occasionally reassign the elders to different families. Without proper oversight from the pastors, a split may occur when an elder takes too much upon himself (see the story of Korah: Numbers 16).

An Elder's Honor
The position of elder within the local church is one of honor. Because of the responsibilities and the hard work of these faithful few, there should be a respect for them in the eyes of the congregation. Elders are part of the authority that God ordained. To show disrespect for an elder is to disrespect God.

1Timothy 5:1 says "Do not rebuke an elder." This is primarily speaking of chronological age, but the principle of respect applies to spiritual elders as well.

Just like pastors, elders are not perfect. If one looks for faults, then faults will be found. If God needed someone perfect to work through then He would have no one besides Jesus. The treasure of the anointing is within earthen vessels (2 Cor. 4:7). God does not say to submit to personalities but to the office. When one's heart is submitted to God, it is possible to submit to someone of personal dislike.

The elder's ministry is part of the pastoral ministry that oversees a church. As such, respect and submission should be shown them by the congregation. They should be recognized as spiritual leaders within the flock.

I Thessalonians 5:12-13 And we urge you brethren, to recognize those who labor among you, and are over you in the Lord and admonish you, and to esteem them very highly in love for their work's sake.

Study Questions, Part 2

1. To rebel against _____ is to rebel against God.

2. To whom has Jesus delegated authority to carry out His purposes in the church?

_____

_____

3. What does *autonomous* mean and how does it relate to church government?

_____

_____

_____

4. What is the proper order in a local churches' *chain of authority*?

_____

_____

_____

5. Why does there need to be a chain of authority in a local church?

_____

_____

_____

_____

6. What is the lead pastor responsible for in the chain or order?

_____

_____

_____

_____

7. What is the role of the pastoral staff within a church?

_____

_____

_____

8. What is the authority of a supportive elder conditional upon? Explain.

_____

_____

_____

_____

_____

9. Are deacons a governmental ministry?

_____

10. Explain what 501(c)3 represents.

_____

_____

_____

11. Who governs the affairs of a non-profit corporation?

_____

12. What are the requirements for a non-profit corporation?

_____

_____

_____

_____

13. What is the difference between the board of directors and the elder's ministry?

_____

_____

_____

14. What was the outcome of the Church council at Jerusalem? What procedure was employed to arrive at this outcome?

_____

_____

_____

_____

_____

15. How many people can one pastor personally minister to and genuinely pastor? What changes have to be made to accommodate further growth?

_____

_____

_____

_____

_____

16. What are some of the responsibilities of an elder towards his assigned families?

_____

_____

_____

_____

_____

17. What should be done if conflict arises between an elder and one of his assigned members?

_____

_____

_____

18. What may be done to avoid church splits from occurring in this system of delegation?

_____

_____

_____

_____

19. What are the four steps involved in dealing with a sinning elder?
1.

_____

_____

2.

_____

_____

3.

_____

_____

4.

_____

_____

20. Explain how one enters the office of an elder, and how one is to leave that same office, if the situation arises. Name the important spiritual principle given.

_____

_____

_____

_____

Section Three: Elders & Deacons

Being, Doing and Placing

I Timothy 3:1 says that if a man desires to have the position of an elder, he desires a "good work." Spiritual leadership is work! If a man is looking for prestige and glamour, he has the wrong impression of the ministry. Many elders have been disillusioned by the expectations that people place upon them. They thought their job was to tell the pastor how to do his job, not to do spiritual work themselves.

Work ethic is something that will not drastically improve *after* one is given the position of an elder. If one has poor work ethics before eldership, he likely will have poor work ethics afterwards also. In the flesh, no one likes to be inconvenienced. Being a spiritual leader in the house of God means being inconvenienced by the problems of those under their care. In the Spirit, an elder sees it not as being inconvenienced, but as ministry. However, to an individual unaccustomed to meeting the needs of others, it can be very stressful work. Some do not have the spiritual, emotional, and mental makeup to be an elder.

There are three distinct phases involved in an individual being placed in as an elder in the local church:

1. **Being**

2. **Doing**

3. **Placing**

Before one can do the work of an elder, there must be a calling, it must be a part of the individual. Calling and being are two aspects of the same work. When an individual acknowledges his calling, the awareness of who he is to be emerges.

Being precedes doing. Being does not come from a title, conversely *doing* does not either. When one is, called to spiritual leadership, it will manifest. An orange tree does not require a sign saying I'm an orange tree – it is identified by the oranges it produces. In a local congregation, there will be those who emerge as leaders by the fruit they produce. Not to say that this happens without proper nurturing and pruning on the part of the pastors, and the Lord Himself (see John 15). However, the calling will be evident by the doing.

Those who say "I'm called to be 'such and such,' please give me the title" are ignorant of the Lord's dealings and consequently show themselves a novice. An orange tree in its early stages may need to be identified by a sign, but after the fruit, its productivity is its calling card. Likewise, if someone is called to a specific spiritual work, in due season the fruit will manifest (Psalm 1:3).

When an individual is doing the work of an elder there should be a special time in which that person is prayed over and publicly placed as an elder. Doing always precedes placing. I can call a door a chair, but I still can't sit in it. The term "elder" is primarily a job description. A chair is a chair because I can sit in it; a door is a door because it opens and closes. An elder is an elder because of spiritual maturity and gifting.

The wrong approach to appointing elders is to assume that because "Joe Believer" is a successful businessman, a good husband and father, and a faithful church attendee, that he is going to be a good elder. While these qualities are admirable, they in and of themselves do not qualify a candidate for eldership. But in many cases "Joe Believer" is approached and appointed and given a list of responsibilities. Out of nowhere he is expected to begin to bear the fruit of an elder. This is often met with frustration on his part, and disappointment on the pastor's end.

The proper approach to appointing elders is to identify those who demonstrate the tendencies and characteristics of a spiritual leader, and develop them. The Bible says that leaders are to give themselves to faithful men (II Tim. 2:2). Train those who apply themselves and raise them up. Work them into leadership as they grow. A title isn't necessary from the outset. When these individuals have come to a place of fruitfulness among the people, in areas of spiritual leadership, bring them before the Body and appoint them as elders. This will release that which has been developed and cause the anointing of God to flow.

An Extension of the Pastor

The ministry of an elder is an extension of the pastor to the congregation; it is not an extension of the congregation to the pastors! In other words, elders are representatives of the pastors and not representatives of the congregation. Faulty church government is the result of reversing this principle.

In studying the ministry of elders one must begin in the Old Testament. The actual function of spiritual elders has not been altered to a great degree from the Old to the New Testament. The ministry of Moses is a prime example of the functioning of elders in a supportive extension capacity. Numbers chapter 11 reveals a frustrated, burnt out leader in Moses. He had been leading the Israelites primarily by himself. He did have the help of

Aaron (spiritually) and Joshua (militarily). But in the day to day affairs and pressures of leadership there was no one to lighten his load.

Numbers 11:15 I am not able to bear all these people all alone, because the burden is too heavy for me.

No one, or even two, pastors can carry the spiritual load of an entire local church. Remember Paul's words concerning his suffering as an apostle: "Apart from all external trials I have the daily burden of responsibility for all the churches" (II Cor. 11:28, Phillip's Translation). External trials come to all of God's people. But there is a demonic attack in the form of pressure that comes only against spiritual leaders. Moses literally asked God to kill him at one point because of this intense pressure (Num. 11:15).

Yet, though there is this type of pressure upon leaders, God's people need guidance from God-appointed leadership. Sheep need shepherds. Moses needed spiritual help to lighten his load.
Many pastors have crumbled under the weight of this spiritual pressure. Moses' answer and the answer for today's pastors is the ministry office of elders functioning in a supportive role as an extension of the pastors to the people.

Listen to God's words to Moses:

> **Numbers 11:16-17**
> **16 So the Lord said to Moses: "Gather to Me seventy men of the elders of Israel, whom you know to be the elders of the people and officers over them; bring them to the tabernacle of meeting, that they may stand there with you.**
> **17 Then I will come down and talk with you there. I will take of the Spirit that is upon you and will put the same upon them; and they shall bear the burden of the people with you, that you may not bear it yourself alone.**

God's answer for Moses was to place the anointing that was on Moses upon the seventy elders. They would then be able to minister to the people in the same sprit as Moses as an extension of his ministry.

Please note these important phrases in the text:

- **"Whom you know"**: You can only work with people on this level that you trust; you can only trust people that you know. The implication is that these men had proved themselves with Moses and with the people.
- **"That they may stand there with you"**: Delegation of leadership responsibility can only occur when there is oneness of purpose. A delegate of authority cannot have his own personal agenda at heart. Pastors need elders that are standing with them! The elders must be behind the vision that God has given the pastor.

Not only is it important to have the same vision of ministry, but it is also important to have the same *philosophy* of ministry. In other words, it is not only important that we agree on where we're going, but also on how we're going to get there. Obviously this is an issue of essentials and not minor details. But what one deems minor may be the cause of ministry shipwreck! Most agree on reaching the lost (vision), but not all agree on *how* to reach them (philosophy). Some may say: "It doesn't matter about philosophy of ministry as long as we have the same spirit." Take warning: where there is a difference of philosophy, there will eventually be a difference of spirit For leadership to flow together, there must be oneness of vision and philosophy.

This vision and philosophy of ministry begins with the lead pastor. The pastoral staff, five-fold ministers, supportive elders, and deacons all must come under the covering of the lead pastor's direction. God said, "I will take of the Spirit that is upon you [Moses] and will put the same upon them [the Elders]." God had given the mantle and anointing of leadership to Moses. When He placed a measure of the same Spirit upon the elders He did not minimize the anointing on Moses. Instead of minimizing the anointing, it served to maximize it! The purpose of elders is not to minimize the leadership of the pastor but for it to be maximized.

God did not take the Spirit that was upon the congregation and put it on the elders to represent the congregation to Moses. God took the Spirit that was upon Moses and put it on the elders to represent Moses to the congregation. As previously stated, the former is false church government.

The primary responsibility of these seventy elders was to bear the burdens of the people. They were burden-bearers. God was not going to stop meeting with Moses on the mount and begin to speak through a committee. Some elder boards have taken Moses off of the mount with God and have lost the glory (see Heb. 8:5 and II Cor. 3:7-8).

Old Testament Elders
The ministry of elders in the New Testament is a carry-over from the Old Testament. As stated, the ministry of spiritual elders has not changed much in function from the Old to the New. A proper understanding of New Testament elders must begin with an Old Testament education of elders.

The Old Testament is filled with men that God rose to prominence in leadership. All of these men utilized the principle that God set forth with Moses. Consider the following examples and their Scripture references:

- Joshua and the elders (Joshua 7:6; 8:10; 24:1, 31; Judges 2:7).
- Samuel and the elders (I Sam. 8:4-7; 15:30). The I Samuel 8:4-7 passage is a prime example of faulty elder government and man-appointed leadership.
- David and the elders (I Chron. 11:3; 15:25; 21:16; 9 Sam. 12:17).
- Solomon and the elders (I Kings 8:1, 3; II Chron. 5:2, 4).
- Ezra and the elders (Ezra 10:1, 8, 14).
- Ezekiel and the elders (Ezek: 8:1; 14: I; 20:1-3). In these passages, God uses Ezekiel to reprove the elders for their idolatry in their heart.

The above elders did not play a prominent role in the ministries of these men. Theirs was a supportive role. I did not say that their role was not important, just not prominent. On many occasions, the above leaders had to deal with a corrupt eldership in Israel. The New Testament teaches us that Israel is our example, that we should learn from their mistakes (I Cor. 10:11). This is why the New Testament gives such strict qualifications for elders.

Pillars of Support

In Chapter One we discussed the matter of the pattern and the glory. The Church must have divine order according to Biblical pattern if it is to contain "the fullness of Him who fills all in all" (Eph. 1:23). It is imperative that things be set in God's order. Part of that order is the setting apart of elders (primarily), and deacons (secondarily).

As an apostle, Paul installed Titus as the overseer of the congregations (many of which were house churches due to a lack of facilities) in Crete. Crete was an island in the Aegean Sea, about 140 miles long and 30 miles wide. His first responsibility was to set things in order by appointing elders in the various churches.

> **Titus 1:5 For this reason I left you in Crete, that you should set in order the things that are lacking, and appoint elders in every city as I commanded you.**

Here we see a clear chain of command: Paul over Titus and Titus over the elders. Paul didn't suggest that Titus set things in order he gave him the directive. Titus was a man in authority, and a man under authority. Notice that Paul said "you" set things in order. He didn't tell him to have a committee meeting about it!

The setting of things in order paved the way for the full expression of the Lord Jesus Christ through His Body at Crete. Churches today are so out of order that little to no expression of Jesus is coming forth. The glory has departed and Ichabod is written over the doors. We must return to the foundation of the apostles and prophets (see Eph. 2:20).

Pillars of Support

Every house needs to be properly upheld. Even a solid foundation is not sufficient if there is nothing to support the structure built thereon. The foundation of the local church is the five-fold ministry (Eph. 2:20), but every church needs pillars to support the house. The word "pillars" is found in Galatians 2:9 and Revelation 3:12.

> **Galatians 2:9 And when James, Cephas, and John, who seemed to be pillars, perceived the grace that had been given to me, they gave me and Barnabas the right hand of fellowship, that we should go to the Gentiles and they to the circumcised.**

> **Revelation 3:12 He who overcomes, I will make him a pillar in the temple of My God, and he shall go out no more. I will write on him the name of My God and the name of the city of My God, the New Jerusalem, which comes down out of heaven from My God. And I will write on him My new name.**

The verse in Galatians is making reference to the apostleship to the Jews. The verse in Revelation is a promise to all who overcome. The term "pillar" aptly fits the ministry function of an elder. It is translated from the Creek word "stulos," meaning "a pillar, a column, a prop or support."

There is a great need in the Body of Christ for pillars. When the pillars are not properly in place there is additional stress and pressure upon the ministry gifts, the foundation. This was the case with Moses in Numbers chapter 11:

Numbers 1.1:14, 16, 17
I am not able to bear all these people alone, because the burden is too heavy for me... So the LORD said to Moses. "Gather to me seventy men of the elders of Israel... I will take of the Spirit that is upon you and will put the sane upon them; and they shall bear the burden of the people with you, that you may not bear it yourself alone.

The same Spirit that was upon Moses came upon the elders. Pillars in the church must have the same Spirit and vision as the pastors to properly bear the burdens of the people. If the pastors continually have to keep division and strife out of the ranks of the elders, the burdens will be increased instead of decreased.

This counsel to have elders assist Moses was first given by his father-in-law Jethro in Exodus 18:18-22:

Exodus 18:
18 Both you and these people who are with you will surely wear yourselves out. For this thing is too much for you; you are not able to perform it by yourself.
19 Listen now to my voice; I will give you counsel, and God will be with you: Stand before God for the people, so that you may bring the difficulties to God.
20 And you shall teach them the statutes and the laws, and show them the way in which they must walk and the work they must do.
21 Moreover you shall select from all the people able men, such as fear God, men of truth, hating covetousness; and place such over them to be rulers of thousands, rulers of hundreds, rulers of fifties, and rulers of tens.
22 And let them judge the people at all times. Then it will be that every great matter they shall bring to you, but every

small matter they themselves shall judge. So it will be easier for you, for they will bear the burden with you.

Several key truths can be gleaned from this "Jethro Principle." Moses was doing all of the counseling and ministering himself, from morning until evening (v. 13). Jethro rightly assessed that it would wear Moses out. He said "This thing is too much for you'" (v. 18). Jethro then proceeded to give Moses a method of operation that would enable Moses to fulfill his calling from God by utilizing his strengths and not allowing his weaknesses to be exploited. Jethro gave a job description for Moses and for the elders that he would choose to assist him.

Moses' Job Description:

1. Stand before God for the people. Bring their difficulties to God (v. 19). Without a strong prayer life, a pastor has nothing to offer but human potential.
2. Teach the people the statutes and laws – the Word of God (v. 20a). The ministry of the Word is the chief ministry of a pastor (see Acts 6:4 concerning the priority of prayer and the Word).
3. Show the people the way in which they must walk and communicate the vision to them (v. 20b). A pastor must possess the heavenly vision (Acts 26:19) and be able to communicate it to the people. Without such they will perish (Prov. 29:18).
4. Show the people the work they must do (v. 20c). It is not enough to communicate the vision. People must be taught practical principles and be trained to do the works of Jesus to carry out the vision.
5. Select able men to appoint as elders (v. 21a). This is no unimportant task. The wrong selection of elders can be the downfall of a previously thriving ministry.

Elder's Job Description

1. The following qualifications had to be met: (a) "able men," (b) "such as fear God," (c) "men of truth," (d) "hating covetousness" (v. 21a).
2. They were delegated authority from Moses to rule according to each one's ability (v. 21b). Some were over thousands, some hundreds, some fifties, and some tens.
3. The elders were counsel the people and make judgment (v. 22a). Small matters were to be handled exclusively by the elders. Every great matter they were to bring to Moses. Elders are an extension of the pastoral ministry in the church. Having the same Spirit (Num. 11:16-17), they are representatives of the pastors.

The end result of this type of facilitation was that the people were better ministered to and no one was neglected. And for Moses: "So it will be easier for you, for they will bear the burden with you" (v. 22b). Elders are called to be burden-bearers and pillars of support.

The Importance of Character
When the pastors begin to choose supportive leadership in the church, there are some important things to watch for. God puts a high premium on character. Charisma and gifting may give good first impressions, but ultimately, character will give a lasting impression.

An individual should use his gift to build the church instead of using the church to build his ministry. Promotion comes from above (Psalm 75). God alone can exalt someone into a position of ministry. Those who strive to be noticed and exalted are the ones God passes over (see Luke 14:12). 1 Peter 5:6 says: "Therefore humble yourselves wider the mighty hand of God that He may exalt you in due time"

The following is a list of some of the character problems that pose a danger when choosing elders and deacons:

- An ambitious spirit; political maneuvers
- Lack of faithfulness in small areas
- An unteachable spirit
- A lack of genuine concern and love for the sheep.
- The lack of a servant's heart
- More love for his/her own ministry, than the well-being of the flock
- Overwhelming charisma, but little action to back it up
- Unethical practices in business and family matters
- Lack of ability to communicate
- An uncooperative attitude
- A spirit of pride; lack of humility
- An undisciplined devotional life in prayer and the Word
- Impure motives, personal agenda
- Mood swings: easily excited and/or discouraged
- Lack of submission to pastors
- Problems and conflicts with previous pastors and churches
- Unwillingness to serve without a title

The terms "Elder" and "Deacon" are primarily job descriptions, rather than titles. Giving someone a title does not "make" them something. Not giving someone a title does not stop them from being something. A desire for positions and titles can be a very unholy motive. Jesus said that if we want to be great, then we must be a servant (Matt. 20:26). Job 32:21-22 warns against flattering titles.

The Terms

There are several Greek words in the New Testament which are translated "elder" or "bishop," though there are only two root words. The term "elder" is from a Hebrew background, while the term "bishop" is of a Greek origin. *Elder* refers more to the spiritual maturity of the individual while *bishop* denotes the actual ministry and job description of the leader One is not a higher position over the other in the New Testament Church. Paul uses the words interchangeably. Both words refer to the same position.

Greek words for and related to "Elder" in the New Testament:

1. **Presbuteros** (adjective): This word is used (a) of age, a person advanced in life, a senior (I Tim. 5:2); (b) of rank or positions of responsibility.

   Presbuteres is used in the Septuagint (Greek translation of the Old Testament) for those who were the leaders of their tribes and families in the Jewish nation. It is the word used for the seventy who assisted Moses (Num. 11):

   In New Testament times, the word was still used of official leaders of the Jewish people. Synagogue rulers were called elders, as were members of the Sanhedrin (see Luke 7:3; Acts 6:12; Luke 4:20).

   Its greatest usage in terms of importance to church government is when applied to leaders in the New Testament Church (Acts 14:23; Titus 1:5). These were individuals who were raised up by the Holy Spirit and appointed by apostolic authority to help oversee the affairs of the local churches (Acts 20:28).

   Presbuteres occurs 66 times in the New Testament.

2. **Sumpresbuteros** (adjective): This word carries the same definition as the above, only it has a prefix attached. The prefix "sum" means "with." *Sumpresbuteros* means "a fellow-elder or co-elder." It is used only once, in I Peter 5:1.

3. **Presbuterion** (noun): "An assembly of aged men, or the order of elders." This word is translated "Presbytery" in I Timothy 4:14. It is applied to a group of elders gathered together in session. This word can be applied to the ministry team of local supportive elders.

   Another application (likely the one referred to in I Timothy 4:14) is to a governing body of apostle-elders, prophet-elders, evangelist-elders, pastor-elders, and teacher-elders that God had knit together in mutual submission. In Timothy's case, they were an ordaining and sending presbytery that retained oversight. In the New Testament, there were primarily two presbytery headquarters:

   - Jerusalem for the Jews
   - Antioch for the Gentiles

   For *Pastoral Church Government* to be in divine order, each pastor should be mutually submitted to other leaders within a presbytery, and when possible to an apostolic authority. An apostle should be the Chairman of the presbytery.

   The word *Presbuterion* occurs three times in the New Testament. The key passage is I Timothy 4:14:

> **Do not neglect the gift that is in you, which was given to you by prophecy with the laying on of the hands of the presbytery [presbuterion].**

Greek words for and related to "Bishop" In the New Testament:

1. **Episkopos**: "An overseer, a superintendent, a guardian." *Episkopos* is a compound word, the preposition "epi" meaning "over" and the word "skopos" meaning "to look or watch, to peer about, to oversee."

   Thayer's Lexicon says: "An overseer, a man charged with the duty of seeing that things to be done by others are done rightly." Wuest's commentary on the Greek says: "The word came originally from secular life, referring to the foreman of a construction gang."

   Jesus Himself is referred to as the "Bishop" of our souls in I Peter 2:25.

   The word is found five times in the New Testament and is translated "overseer" (Acts 20:28) and "Bishops" (Phil. 1:1; I Tim. 3:2; Tit. 1:7; I Pet. 2:25).

2. **Episkope**: The noun form of *episkopos*. It means "inspection, investigation, visitation, oversight." This word is very telling concerning the responsibility of an elder. Visiting the sheep and giving oversight into their spiritual life is a key responsibility of elders.

   The word is translated: "Bishoprick" (Arts 1:20), "Bishop" (I Tim. 3:1), and "Visitation" (I Pet. 2:12).

3. **Eplskopeo**: The verb form of *episkopos*. It means "to oversee; by implication, to beware." *Episkopeo* is translated: "looking diligently" (Heb.12:15) and "take the oversight" (I Pet. 5:2).

Qualifications for Elders

The Word of God is very clear concerning the qualifications and requirements for an elder. In this section, I will cover the lists of qualifications that Paul gave for elders in I Timothy 3 and Titus 1. In covering these qualifications, I will give the student several translations to compare.

Before an individual is set apart for the work of an elder, it is important that there be a time of proving. I Timothy 3:10 says: "But let these also first be proved," referring to deacons. However, the word "also" is referring to elders. Elders must go through a time of proving before responsibility is charged to them. The word "proved" is the Greek word "dokimazo." *Dokimazo* means "to try, prove, discern, distinguish, approve. It has the notion of proving a thing whether it be worthy to be received or not. The Weymouth translation renders it "probation." This is clearly what Paul had in mind. Putting someone in a position before they are ready can be harmful to both the flock and the individual.

The Word is silent as to how long this proving or probation time should be. However, wisdom and experience teach that it should be at least six months to a year after they meet the qualifications. This time-frame will vary, but not greatly. It may take longer than a year with those who have moral and character deficiencies in their background.

The elder qualifications of I Timothy 3 and Titus 1 fall into three categories:

    A. Character
    B. Domestic
    C. Spiritual

A. Character Qualifications

1. **An elder is to be blameless** (I Tim. 3:2; Tit. 1:6). The Amplified Bible says: "must give no grounds for accusation but must be above reproach." Knox translation says: "must be one with whom no fault can be found"

2. **An elder is to be temperate** (I Tim. 3:2; Tit. 1:8). This word means self-control. An elder should not have a problem with excess in any area of his life. This is especially important in regards to appetites and affections.

3. **An elder is to be sober** (I Tim. 3:2; Tit. 1:8). An elder is not to be irrational. He should be prudent and sensible. This word also carries the meaning of "being discreet" An elder must be able to keep a confidence. One note: soberness is not sadness. Other translations include:

   - "Serious-minded" - The New Testament in Basic English.
   - "Prudent" - The New American Standard
   - "Discreet" - Twentieth Century New Testament

4. **An elder is to be of good behavior** (I Tim. 3:2). The Greek word "kosmios" carries the meaning "being orderly and modest." An

elder is always before the scrutinizing eyes of the people. Leadership is a fish-bowl type existence. The elder's behavior must be unquestionable. Other translations include:

1. "Well-ordered life" - TCNT
2. "An orderly [disciplined] life" – Amplified

5. **An elder is not to be given to wine** (I Tim. 3:3; Tit. 1:7). This would include any form of intoxication. Wine was a common drink in Bible days; some was fermented, some unfermented. The fermented was less than 2% alcohol; it would have taken lots of it to get drunk. The literal translation says: "not tarrying at or staying near wine.

6. **An elder is not to be a violent** (I Tim. 3:3; Tit. 1:7). The elder's battles are not to be fought in the flesh (Eph. 6:12). The Greek word for violent is "plektes" it means "quarrelsome, one ready to strike back at those who displease him." Some other renderings are as follows:

- "Not combative" – Amplified
- "Not ready to wound" – Emphasized New Testament

7. **An elder is not to be greedy for money** (I Tim. 3:3; Titus 1:7). Money should never be the motivation for life's decisions. The love of money is the root of all sorts of evil (I Tim.6:10). The Greek word for "greedy for money" (*aischkrokerde*) means "not desirous of base gain; not using wrong methods to raise money to increase his own income."

8. **An elder Is to be gentle (patient)** (I Tim. 3:3). However spiritual and anointed one may be, being an elder is still primarily dealing with people. Gentleness and patience is one of the greatest

needs for an elder. Without this quality, one's ministry will be stopped short of lasting success.

Some other translations of this word are: "forbearing" (American Bible Union); "considerate" (Emphasized N.T.); "peaceable" (Conybeare).

9. **An elder is not to be quarrelsome** (I Tim. 3:3; Tit. 1:7). An argumentative person is not qualified to be an elder. Titus' rendering of this qualification is "not quick tempered" It is one thing to disagree with someone; it is another to want to argue over every point of disagreement. An elder must be non-contentious. Some other translations are as follows:

- "Not contentious" - American Standard Version
- "Avoiding quarrels" - New English Bible
- "Not be a controversialist" - Phillips Translation

10. **An elder is not to be covetous** (I Tim. 3:3). The elder's desires should be toward spiritual things, not temporal things. The Greek word for "covetous" (*aphilarguros*) means "not a lover of money, not desiring the office for the sake of personal gain." Eldership is not to be viewed as a stepping stone to further one's personal ministry. God may in fact use it as such, but to view it that way in our motives is a disqualifying factor!

11. **An elder is not to be self-willed** (Tit. 1:7). Self-will caused the fall of Lucifer (examine the five "I will..." statements of Lucifer in Isa. 14:13-14). A man with an "I" problem is disqualified from eldership. A man who insists on his own way is not open to God's way! Other translations include:

- "Not stubborn" - New Testament in the Language of the People
- "Not arrogant" - New Testament an American Translation
- "Not overbearing" - NEB

12. **An elder is to be a lover of good** (Tit. 1:8). An elder never has anything good to say about the practice of evil. There should be no desire for things which are evil, unrighteous, or even questionable. This also speaks to attitude. An elder should have a positive outlook, seeing the glass half-full rather than half-empty.

13. **An elder is to have a good testimony with outsiders** (I Tim. 3:7). An elder must have an excellent testimony and reputation with unbelievers in the community. This includes areas of financial obligations; business dealings; community relations; legal matters; taxes, etc. In secular employment, it is important for an elder to have the respect of his co-workers; he should not be slothful or critical of supervisors. An elder is an example outside of the church as well as within. Other translations include:

- "Well-spoken of by outsiders" - TCNT
- "Bear a good character, too, in the world's eyes." - Knox translation

B. Domestic Qualifications

1. **An elder must be the husband of one wife** (I Tim. 3:2; Tit. 1:6). This qualification does not specifically involve divorce and/or remarriage, though the two may relate. An eider must be a loyal husband without adulterous relationships or attitudes. The Greek for this qualification is *mias gunaikos* meaning "of one woman." A literal translation would be a one-woman husband." An elder should be totally

dedicated to his wife and not flirtatious. This qualification does not disqualify single men or women; the Apostle Paul himself was single. Other translations of this phrase include:

- "One wife's husband - Berkeley Version
- "Faithful to his one wife" - NEB

2. **An elder is to be hospitable** (I Tim. 3:2; Tit. 1:3). This Greek word (*philozenon*) means "a lover of strangers." An elder must get involved in people's lives on a personal level; this includes having them in his home and visiting them in theirs. An elder should help "the least" as commanded by Jesus in Matthew 25:34-40.

3. **An elder is to rule his own house well** (I Tim. 3:4-5; Tit. 1:6).

> **I Timothy 3:4-5**
> **4 one who rules his own house well, having his children in submission with all reverence**
> **5 (for if a man does not know how to rule his own house, how will he take care of the church of God?)**
>
> **Titus 1:6 Having faithful children not accused of dissipation or insubordination.**

An elder must preside over and manage the affairs of his household well. An elder's house must be in order according to the Word of God (see I Cor. 11:3-12; Eph. 5:22-32). The man is to be the head of the home. However, headship is not dictatorship. Headship involves concern and care and provision. The man is responsible for the overall direction of the family. An elder must not guilty of heading the voice of his wife above the voice of the Lord (Gen. 3:17). Other translations include:

- "Able to manage his own household properly" – Moffatt's translation
- "He must be one who is a good head to his own family" - Knox

The elder ruling his house well involves two primary areas: (a) his wife and (b) his children.

A. **The Elder's Wife**: While there are no qualifications listed for the elder's wife, there are for the deacon's wife (I Tim. 3:11). A deacon's wife must have these qualifications; therefore, it is implied that an elder's wife must also qualify. These qualifications include:

  1. **Reverent:** This means "venerable, honorable, honest."
  2. **Not Slanderous:** Greek: "diabolis," meaning "to give false report injure another by defaming." This is the Greek word translated "Devil."
  3. **Temperate:** Self-control and discipline (see A.2 above).
  4. **Faithful in an all things:** The elder's wife should be reliable, trustworthy, and dependable.

B. **The Elder's Children**: Children are a reflection of the quality of home life. Continuous upheaval in public is a sure sign that the home is not in order. The following are qualifications for elder's children:

1. **An elder's children should be in submission** (I Tim. 3:4). The Amplified says: "Keeping his children under control, with true dignity, commanding their respect in every way and keeping them respectful.

2. **An elder's children should have reverence** (I Tim. 3:4). The children of an elder must show respect for authority: parents, church leadership, the house of God, teachers, civil authorities, etc.

3. **An elder's children should be faithful** (Tit. 1:6). The Amplified Bible says: "whose children are [well trained and are] believers." It is the parent's responsibility to train up a child in the way he should go. (Prov. 22:6).

4. **An elder's children should not be accused of riot** (Tit. 1:6). Unrestrained behavior, wild, rowdy.

5. **An elder's children should not be insubordinate.** (Tit. 1:6). Disorderly, rebellious, uncontrollable, badly behaved. One translation renders it "unwillingness to obey" (New Testament a New Translation).

A man's first ministry is to his family. If an elder keeps this perspective, other things will come into place. However, there are certain situations where an elder has no control over the actions of a family member. We cannot control the will of another human being. Matters of this nature should be dealt with on an individual basis. In order to disqualify someone on the basis of the actions of another, the instance would have to be a direct result of the elder's lack of responsibility.

C. Spiritual Qualifications

1. **An elder must be able to teach** (I Tim. 3:2). This does not mean that all elders have the ministry gift of teaching, but that all elders should be "apt" (KJV) to teach. There are different levels of teaching: large groups, small groups,

personal, etc. An elder should be knowledgeable in the Word of God, and be able to proclaim and expound its truths. This might include:

- Filling in for the pastor
- Teaching small groups
- Teaching Sunday school
- New converts class
- Personal counseling

The Berkeley Version renders it "qualified to teach"

2. An elder must not be a novice or a new convert (I Tim 3:6). A leader that lacks experience is unqualified to lead God's people. Moses first had to spend 40 years on the backside of the desert before he was able to lead God's people for 40 years. The call may come in the novice stage, even anointing, but these in themselves are not sufficient grounds for setting apart. Paul was not separated to the office of an apostle until he had been saved for 10 years (Acts 13).

The word "novice" also means "newly planted." A believer that is new   a congregation should not be immediately placed into leadership. He must first learn to submit to the present leadership and the vision of the pastors; then he can be brought in after a time of faithfulness and proving.

Any mature believer with a call to eldership will not desire an immediate position upon joining a new church.

3. **An elder is to be just** (Tit. 1:8). Not only being in right standing with God, but also doing right before God in

dealings with other people. Right conduct in accordance with the Biblical standard.

4. **An elder is to be holy** (Tit. 1:8). Holiness is not a suggestion in the Word of God-it is a command! Hebrews 12:14 says, "And holiness, without which no one will see the Lord" An elder is called to be an example to the flock. Holiness in spirit, attitude and deed is one of the greatest requirements for leadership in the Body of Christ. Carnality cannot be permitted to rule in an elder's life. This word "holy" carries the connotation of being sanctified and set apart for the Master's use.

5. **An elder must hold fast the faithful word as he has been taught.** (Tit. 1:9). There are many things which come to try to steal the Word of God from our hearts; an elder must hold fast. Elders should be taught by the pastors and ministry staff of the church. Imparting the Word and the vision to future leaders is the most valuable investment any pastor can make. An elder must prove himself in this area of holding fast in times of testing.

   A pastor should ask this question concerning the candidate for eldership: "Does this brother put the Word of God into practice in his personal life, or is he a hearer of the Word only?" (see James 1:22).

   Other translations include:

   • "And a man who continues to cling to the trustworthy message" - New Testament in the Language of the People

- "He must hold by the sure truths of doctrine" - Moffatt's translation

6. **An elder must be able to exhort and convict by sound doctrine** (Tit. 1:9). There are many insubordinate people in the church (Tit. 1:10); an elder must be able to carry an authority to convict, but also must be loving enough to exhort. This is accomplished through the Word of God, not in the flesh.

There are many winds of doctrine that try to blow into the church (Eph. 4:14). Elders who know the Word of God are one of the greatest safeguards against it (see Acts 20:28-29).

The Ministry of Elders

The Bible teaches us that there are "diversities of gifts, differences of ministries, and diversities of operations" (I Cor. 12:4-6). God deals with churches individually. What the New Testament gives us is a skeletal outline of church government. Without the life and anointing of the Holy Spirit, it becomes dead formalism with no power. The gift ministries and operations of God will vary slightly from church to church, but the basic concepts will remain the same.

In this chapter I will list the many ministries and functions of an elder. No one should be given a job without a thorough job description. One cannot be held accountable to do what one does not know to do. This is a major cause of frustration among church leaders: "What exactly is my job?"

The following list is not exhaustive but thorough. Some churches may have no need for certain ministries listed; some may have additional ministry needs not listed here. Each church should personally adapt a job description for the elder's ministry.

This list is not necessarily given in the order of importance. Importance is determined by need and needs vary from church to church. Scripture references will be given when available and applicable.

The Ministry of Visitation: Remember the sheep that is turned upon its back cannot turn itself upright; it will stay in that position until rescued, or it dies. Elders should be involved in visiting absentees from services.

> **Jeremiah 23:2 (KJV) Therefore thus saith the Lord God of Israel against the pastors that feed my people; Ye have scattered my flock, and driven them away, and have not visited them: behold, I will visit upon you the evil of your doings, saith the Lord.**

Newcomers and new converts should be contacted within 48 hours. Reports should be made back to the pastoral staff. Consider the following statistics:

- First-time visitors who eventually make that church their home church: 10% to 12%
- Second-time visitors: 25% to 28%
- Third-time visitors: 40% to 45%

As can be clearly seen, getting a first-time visitor to come back for a second week doubles the chances of their becoming a permanent member.

The Ministry of Correction and Discipline: Sin in the camp keeps the church from doing great exploits for God. Sin is self-destructive, but also blights the testimony of the Church of Christ. When a member is in sin, the church cannot look the other way. This would be sinning against our offending brother. Elders must be able to correct in love for the purpose of restoration. There are times when restoration is not immediately possible and excommunication is the only recourse.

The New Testament lists 16 reasons for excommunication:

1. Refusing to make peace (Matt. 18:15-17)
2. Causing divisions and strife (Rom. 16:17)
3. Fornication (I Cor. 5:11-13)
4. Covetousness (I Cor. 5:11-13)
5. Idolatry (I Cor. 5:11-13)
6. Trouble making (I Cor. 5:11-13)
7. Drunkenness (I Cor. 5:11-13)
8. Extortion (I Cor. 5:11-13)
9. Refusal to love God (I Cor. 16:22)
10. Unbelief, infidelity (II Cor. 6:14)
11. Backsliding (II Cor. 13:1-2,10)
12. Disorderly conduct (II Thes. 3:6)
13. Defying the truth (II Thes 3:14)
14. Denying the faith (I Tim. 1:19-20)
15. False teaching (I Tim. 6:3-5; II John 10)
16. Being a heretic (Tit. 3:10-11)

The foremost goal with all of these sins, however, is restoration.

The Ministry of Restoration: As stated, even in the above mentioned cases, the goal is always restoration. The sinning member at Corinth that was excommunicated from fellowship was later restored after repentance. The leadership was instructed by Paul to:

a) Forgive him
b) Comfort him
c) Reaffirm their love to him

(See II Cor. 2:6-9).

The elder's ministry will center in large part around this ministry of restoration.

Galatians 6:1 Brethren, if a man is overtaken in any trespass, you who are spiritual restore such a one in a spirit of gentleness, considering yourself lest you also be tempted.

Also see Matthew 18:15

The Ministry of Teaching: As previously expounded, all five-fold teachers are elders, but all elders do not stand in the office of teacher. Even so, I Timothy 3:2 says, "A bishop then must be... able to teach." There are different levels of teaching. If not a five-fold minister, an elder should still be able to teach on a personal or small group level.

The Ministry of Small Groups: A small group, sometimes called a cell group, is a group of 10-15 believers within a local church that gather in a home for worship, fellowship, prayer, and teaching. This gives church members an opportunity build stronger relationships within the larger body. This ministry has enhanced church growth in many churches. However, this should only be done under the supervision of authority, namely an elder. The elder should oversee the gatherings and outreaches. He should also be the primary instructor in the teaching time.

The early church practiced corporate, public worship, but also met in houses to break bread and fellowship: "So continuing daily with one accord in the temple, and breaking bread from house to house" (Acts 2:46).

The Ministry of Intercession: Elders are called upon to be spiritual watchmen (Isa. 62:6-7). Prayer for the pastoral staff and the flock should be without ceasing (Eph. 6:18). There are many snares in the ministry; intercession by supportive elders will prevent Satan from succeeding in his schemes. The greatest service that anyone can perform for their leaders is to pray for them in earnest.

In times of discouragement, or after a time of defeat in the camp, it is especially important that elders stand with their leaders in prayer. After Israel's defeat at the hands of Ai, Joshua and the elders interceded together: "Then Joshua tore his clothes, and fell to the earth on his face before the ark of the LORD until evening, the elders of Israel" (Joshua 7:6).

The Ministry of Protection: There are many enemies to the flock. One of the primary roles of elders is to guard the flock of God. An elder is likened unto a sheep dog in that a sheep dog keeps the sheep in the fold and the wolves out.

Paul never gave a more serious admonition than he did to the elders of Ephesus: "Take heed to yourselves and to all the flock... For I know this, that after my departure savage wolves will come in among you, not sparing the flock" (Acts 20:28-29).

After Paul gave Titus the qualifications for elders (Tit. 1:6-9), he immediately gave one of their primary   duties: "For there are many insubordinate... whose mouths must be stopped" (Titus 1:10-11). Elders are responsible for silencing those who are rebellious towards leadership.

The Ministry of Advice: Even though the human body has only one head, it still listens to the information of the five senses before making decisions. Elders are like those five senses throughout the body, relaying back information to the head. To ignore what the senses are saying can result in the loss of life. I Kings 12:6-8, 13 should be examined to find out what happens when a leader is unteachable and will not receive counsel.

Elders do not control pastors, for they are subservient. However, they have been given as a blessing to the pastoral gift. Proverbs

11:14 says, "Where there is no counsel, the people fall; But in the multitude of counselors there is safety."

Sometimes the advice of elders is wrong. In those cases, a pastor should have the backbone to follow the instruction of the Lord. However, for the most part, if the elders are chosen by God, there will be harmony in the decision-making process. The final say is ultimately the lead pastors (Acts 15:19). At that point, unless its unscriptural, immoral or unethical, the elders should give their full support.

The Ministry of Evangelism and Discipleship: As examples to the congregation, elders must maintain a lifestyle of soul-winning and evangelism. When the congregation sees their leaders sharing the gospel with neighbors and co-workers it will inspire them to do likewise.

The Great Commission commands: "Go therefore and make disciples of all the nations... teaching them to observe all things that I have commanded you" (Matt 28:19-20). Paul told Timothy, the ruling elder at Ephesus, to "do the work of an evangelist" (II Tim. 4:5). All believers, especially leaders as Timothy, are called to the primary task of an evangelist – to win souls. This does not require one to stand in the office of an evangelist.

After conversion, new converts need to be discipled. Left alone they will revert to earlier behavior patterns; their minds need renewed (Rom. 12:2). Elders should take extra measures to work with the new converts in the congregation. Attention should be given to their attendance, their struggles, and their progress. Elders should be available for counseling those new to the faith.

The Ministry of Counseling: Part of tending the flock of God is ministering to their personal needs. This is the area that Moses was getting burnt out on, trying to fix every one's problems (see Num. 11). He couldn't do it on his own. One or two pastors cannot tend to the personal needs of an entire congregation. The elder's staff must be available for counseling.

One trap that the elders must stay aware of is that if what I call people who choose to be "permanent problem people." In other words, they don't want to actually do anything about their problem. Often it is a case of blame shifting – i.e., taking no personal accountability themselves. Once this problem has been identified, counseling must be discontinued until the individual is willing to make changes. Otherwise it becomes a trap to the elder, draining him spiritually so that he is of no help to those who truly want to change. An elder must develop discernment to know the difference between people with a problem and problem people.

Certain counseling policies should be set by the lead pastor so that this and other types of abuse do not take place. Counseling of the opposite sex should be done with one's spouse or another elder of the counselee's gender. The pastoral staff should be briefed on all of the counseling taking place within the church.

One of the names of Jesus is "Counselor" (Isa. 9:6). When the focus is not upon Him, nothing will be accomplished. The discerning of spirits is especially valuable in the counseling ministry.   Sometimes deliverance is needed, sometimes just a healthy dose of repentance.

The Ministry of Administration: Though the Church is not a business, and shouldn't be operated as one, there are many business practices that the Church must carry out. More and more, the government is interfering with church matters. Accurate records must be kept to meet government regulations. As well, financial administration has much to do with the-success or failure of a church.

The Bible clearly states that administration is a spiritual gift: "And God has appointed these in the church: first apostles, second prophets, third teachers, after that miracles, then gifts of healings, administration, varieties of tongues" (I Cor. 12:28). Often one or more elders will demonstrate these administrative gifts. This in turn will free the pastors up from such administrative duties and give increase to their anointing.

The Ministry of Sunday School Superintendence: The Christian education of children is a priority ministry in the House of God. One of the main avenues of this goal is the Sunday School program. An elder should take on this supervisory role.

Superintendence may include:

a) Recruiting and training teachers for all age groups.
b) Finding replacement teachers on short notice.
c) Keeping the teachers enthused and current with fresh ideas.
d) Problem solving and conflict resolution.
e) Ordering and screening curriculum (generally on a quarterly basis).
f) Being creative in utilizing space, materials, and workers for maximum output.

Proverbs 22:6 says: "Train up a child in the way he should go, and when he is old he will not depart from it"

The Ministry of being a Department Head: Every ministry within the church needs to be headed up and supervised, much like the Sunday School department above. The word "bishop" means "to oversee." Some of the ministries that need the oversight of elders include:

- Evangelism and outreach
- Ushering and greeting
- Visitation: hospital and shut-in
- Cell groups
- Prayer ministry
- New converts ministry
- Deacons' ministry
- Counseling ministry
- Financial administration

These and other areas of ministry need the supervision of elders. The elders remain under the supervision of the pastor at all times.

The Ministry of Praying for the Sick: James 5:14-15 says, "Is anyone among you sick? Let him call for the elders of the church, and let them pray over hint anointing him with oil in the name of the Lord. And the prayer of faith will save the sick, and the Lord will raise him up. And if he has committed sins, he will be forgiven."

All believers are to lay hands on the sick (Mark 16:18), but elders are called upon emphatically to minister to the sick.

The Ministry of the Gifts of the Spirit: I Corinthians 12:8-10 lists the nine gifts or manifestations of the Spirit: word of wisdom, word of knowledge, faith, gifts of healings, working of miracles, prophecy, discerning of spirits, different kinds of tongues, and interpretation of tongues.

These gifts are available to all believers, as verse seven says, "But the manifestation of the Spirit is given to each one for the profit of all." Elders are called upon to minister to people continually. The gifts of the Spirit cut past the outer problems and go to the root, manifesting the "secrets of the heart" (I Cor. 14:25). More can be accomplished by the power of the Holy Spirit in five minutes than man can accomplish on his own all week! Elders should earnestly desire the gifts, and operate them in love (I Cor. 12:3 1).

The Ministry of Deliverance: Those on the front lines of leadership must know their authority in Christ. When Jesus sent out the twelve disciples He gave them power over unclean spirits (Matt. 10:1). Demons will oppose the going forth of the gospel. The first sign that Jesus said would follow a believer when they went out to preach the gospel was casting out demons (Mark 16:15-17).

Elders must be spiritually prepared to minister to the oppressed and possessed. The devil does not play games. An elder who is not prepared to confront demon power should not be an elder.

The Ministry of Serving Communion: While it is not believed by this pastor that *only* elders can serve communion in the House of the Lord, it is certainly one of their functions. An elder should carefully study I Corinthians 11:23-32. If it is to be *received* in a worthy manner, it must also be served with reverence.

In both the receiving and serving of communion it is imperative that there be no unconfessed sin or unforgiveness in the heart. Elders must keep their hearts pure of the defilement of bitterness and resentment.

The Ministry of Baptizing: Jesus not only gave the commandment to preach the gospel, but to baptize those who believe (Matt.28:19). Whenever possible, baptism should be done publicly by church leadership. Baptism serves as identification with the death, burial, and resurrection of our Lord. It also serves as identification with His body; this is why it best done by church leaders.

Baptism should be done "in the name of the Father and of the Son and of the Holy Spirit" (Matt. 28:19). "In the authority of the Name of Jesus" may be added according to Acts 2:38.

Baptism may be administered in the following way (quoted from the "Christian Minister's Manual" p. 81): "The pool of water should be waist deep. The administrator stands to the left side and somewhat to the rear of the candidate. With his left hand, he grasps the right wrist of the candidate, allowing the latter's hand to be free to hold a handkerchief to cover the nose and mouth. The candidate, with his left hand, grasps the minister's wrist."

"With his right hand upraised, the minister pronounces the charge; then placing his hand between the candidate's shoulders, he lowers the candidate gently backward until the head is completely under the water, he then lifts him up out of the water. The minister should lift with his right hand to avoid pulling the candidate's hand away from his nose and mouth, causing him to swallow water."

Note: If in a stream, the candidate should stand with his back to the current.

The Ministry of Giving: Romans 12:8 specifically lists *giving* as a spiritual ministry. Many times an elder will have this function. Sometimes people in the congregation get jealous over an elder that financially gives and supports the church and the pastors. They can't conceive that the position was not "bought" by the elder's giving. Those with the genuine ministry of giving have no strings attached!

While all elders do not have the specific gift of giving, all elders should be exemplary in their giving practices. Financial wealth is not a prerequisite for eldership, but everyone must give according as God has prospered.

The Ministry of Encouragement: I list this one last but it is certainly not least! Without encouragement, leaders would often give up, or never reach their full potential. Who knows where Paul would have ended up if not for the obedience of Ananias (Acts 9:10-17), and the encouragement of Barnabas (Lit. "Son of Encouragement). See Acts 9:27; 11:25-26.

Elders should encourage their pastor by: a) praying for him; b) publicly supporting and even defending him; c) spending time with him; d) helping them; and e) speaking words of faith and encouragement to his vision.

In King David's time of despair, pleading with God for the life of his son, II Samuel 12:17 says, "So the elders of his house arose and went to him to raise him up from the ground..."

These and other ministries are valuable to the building up of the church. According to the needs and vision of each individual church, some will be more prominent than others. The lead pastor should develop a personalized job description for the elder's ministry that best suits his church.

Appointment and Terms of Elders

It is important to understand how one enters the office of a supportive elder, as well as how one leaves that same office, if the situation arises. Supportive elders are God-gifted but man-called. Let me clarify that: the gifts that make one suitable to be an elder are given by God, but the appointment is not divine, on the level of a five-fold calling. Concerning the five-fold ministry, the Word says, "And He Himself gave some to be apostles, some prophets, some evangelists, and some pastors and teachers" (Eph. 4:11). This type of appointment by God Himself is never connected with supportive elders in the local church. How then are supportive elders appointed? Acts 14:23 and Titus 1:5 answer this question.

> **Acts 14:23**
> **So when they [Paul and Barnabas] had appointed elders in every church, and prayed with fasting, they commended them to the Lord in whom they had believed.**

> **Titus 1:5**
> **For this reason I [Paul] left you [Titus] in Crete, that you should set in order the things that are lacking, and appoint elders in every city as I commanded you.**

It is clear from these two verses that elders are chosen and appointed by the office of the pastor and/or apostle.

The term of an elder is indefinite unless certain circumstances develop. These conditions include:

- Sin in the elder's life
- Unfaithfulness to church
- Insubordination to the pastor and/or staff
- An elder's lack of desire and commitment to continue in the office

Other situations may also occur which necessitates the removal of an elder, such as physically moving from the area.

It is within the pastor's responsibilities to appoint or dismiss an elder for legitimate reasons. As we will see in the module on elders, removal is not to be done based on the elder not being a "yes man." God is not looking for yes men, nor are godly pastors. But when legitimate reasons develop, removal should be done by the pastor. He that appoints you is over you in the Lord. Hebrews 13:17 says, "Obey those who rule over you, and be submissive" An important spiritual principle remains: he who has the authority to appoint you has the authority to remove you.

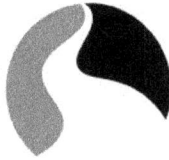

Qualifications for Deacons

The ministry of deacons is vital to the operation of the New Testament Church. The modern church has deviated greatly from the New Testament with regards to the role of deacons. God did not set deacons in place within the church to rule and govern. But sadly, many churches today are run and governed by deacon boards. This goes against the very definition of the word "deacon," which means to serve. It primarily deals with the physical aspects of service.

Paul wrote to the Philippian church and addressed them by saying: "To all the saints in Christ Jesus who are in Philippi, with the bishops and deacons" (Phil. 1:1). Some churches have employed one office to the exclusion of the other. The New Testament Church had both offices functioning simultaneously. One is primarily a spiritual service (elders, i.e., bishops); the other, a physical service (deacons).

While the office of the deacon is primarily a physical service, it is, however, extremely valuable to the spiritual ministry of the Church. Without the physical aspects of church life being taken care of, the spiritual needs could not be adequately met. In the most basic of ways, all Christians are called to be deacons; for deaconship is a life of service. All are called to serve. All are called to have the spirit of a deacon, though all are not called to the office of a deacon. In Paul's salutation to the Philippians he calls himself a "servant of Jesus Christ" (Phil. 1:1). Though Paul was an apostle, he never stopped being a servant. Jesus Christ, Himself, set forth the greatest example of servanthood for us to follow.

Jesus Christ: Pattern Servant
Mark 10:43-45 Yet it shall not be so among you; but whoever desires to become great among you shall be your servant. And whoever of you desires to be first shall be slave of all. For even the Son of Man did not come to be served, but to serve, and to give His life a ransom for many.

Christ is the supreme example of servanthood and deaconship. His was an attitude of humility and servanthood. To be great in God's kingdom is not a matter of getting "high enough," but getting "low enough." God can only use those with servant's hearts. Christ displayed this servant's heart at all times, though He was the Master of the universe.

Philippians 2:5-8 speaks of the humiliation of Christ:

5 Let this mind be in you which was also in Christ Jesus,
6 who being in the form of God did not consider it robbery to be equal with God,
7 but made Himself of no reputation, taking the form of a servant, and coming in the likeness of men,
8 And being found in appearance as a man, He humbled Himself and became obedient to the point of death, even the death of the cross.

Jesus Christ laid aside the divine attributes of the Godhead to come to earth as a man. He remained God, while limiting Himself to the capabilities of a man, anointed with the Holy Spirit (Acts 10:38). He was and is 100% God and 100% man. It is the miracle of the incarnation. While living as a man, Jesus did not seek to make a reputation for Himself. What a stark contrast this is for many modem preachers. Instead of making themselves of no reputation, many have hired press agents and public relations firms to promote their ministries. Just a stroll through the latest edition of a current charismatic publication will testify of this trend. Jesus always relegated Himself to the position of servant.

Consider John chapter 13 for the greatest example of servanthood ever. It is not just that Jesus bowed down and washed the disciple's feet; this was example enough. But among the twelve was Judas Iscariot, the betrayer. Jesus, knowing that Judas was only hours away from ultimate betrayal, bowed down and washed Judas' feet! Jesus was leaving an example of servanthood for all to follow.

> **John 13:**
> **13 You call Me Teacher and Lord, and you say well, for so I am. 14 If I then, your Lord and Teacher, have washed your feet, you also ought to wash one another's feet.**
> **15 For I have given you an example, that you should do as I have done to you.**
> **16 Most assuredly, I say to you, a servant is not greater than his master; nor is he who is sent greater than he who sent him.**

Defining the Terms

While there is only one Greek root word for "deacon" in the New Testament, that Greek word is translated several different ways. "Deacon" is not found in the Old Testament, for its original concept is based in the New Testament. However, a parallel may be found between deacons and the Levites of the Old Testament.

There are three Greek words for, or related to, the word "deacon." All three have the same root.

1. **Diakonos** (noun): "A servant of the people, a waiter, an attendant, a servant or minister." This word is used 32 times in the Greek text. The King James Version translates *diakonos* in the following ways:

   - "Deacon" 5 times (Phil. 1:1; I Tim. 3:8, 10, 12, 13)
   - "Servant" 7 times (Matt. 22:13; 23:11; Mark 9:35; John 2:5, 9; 12:26; Rom. 16:1)
   - "Minister" 20 times (Matt. 20:26; Mark 10:43; Romans 13:4; 15:8; I Cor. 3:5; etc.)

2. **Diakonia** (noun): "Serviceable labor, assistance, a service or ministry to the people." This word is used 34 times in the Greek text. *Diakonos* refers more to the person, *diakonia* to the office. The King James Version translates *diakonia* in the following ways:

   - "Ministry" 16 times (Acts 1:17, 25; 6:4; 12:25; 20:24; 21:19; etc.)
   - "Ministration" 6 times (Acts 6:1; II Cor. 3:7, 8, 9; 9:13)
   - "Ministering" 3 times (Rom. 12:7; II Cor. 8:4; 9:1)
   - "Service" 2 times (Rom. 15:31; II Cor. 11:8)
   - "Administration" 2 times (I Cor. 12:5; II Cor. 9:12)
   - "Serving," "relief," "office," "do service," "to minister" all once (Luke 10:40; Acts 11:29; Rom. 11:13; II Cor. 11:8; Heb. 1:14)

3. **Diakoneo** (verb): "To serve, to wait upon, to care for someone's needs." This word is used 37 times in the Greek New Testament. The King James Version translates *diakoneo* in the following ways:

- "Minister unto" 15 times (Matt. 4:11; 8:15; 20:28; 25:44; Mark 10:45; Luke 8:3; II Tim. 1:18; etc.)
- "Serve" 10 times (Luke 10:40; 12:37; 17:8; John 12:2, 26; Acts 6:2; etc.)
- "Minister" 7 times (Matt. 20:28; Mark 10:45; 2 Cor. 3:3; I Pet. 1:12; 4:10, 11)
- "Administer" 2 times (II Cor. 8:19, 20)
- "Use the office of a deacon" 2 times (I Tim. 3:10, 13).
- "Minister to" once (Heb. 6:10).

One can clearly see the implications of this word by how the King James translators rendered it. The words *diakonos*, *diakonia* and *diakoneo* are frequently used outside of the formal office of deacon. All are called to have the servant's heart of a deacon, but all are not called to the office of a deacon in the local church. Certain qualifications and requirements must be met for this to occur.

Qualifications for a Deacon

The Word of God is very clear concerning the qualifications and requirements for a deacon. In this section I will cover the list of qualifications that Paul gave for deacons in I Timothy chapter three. In covering these qualifications, I will give the reader several translations to compare.

Before an individual is set apart for the work of a deacon, it is important that, there be a time of proving. I Timothy 3:10 says "But let these also first be proved," referring to deacons. The word "proved" is the Greek word *dokimazo*, which means, "to try, prove, discern, distinguish, approve." It has the notion of proving a thing whether it be worthy to be received or not." The Weymouth translation renders it "probation." This is clearly what Paul had in mind. Putting someone in a position before they are ready can be harmful to both the flock and the individual.

The Word is silent as to how long this proving or probation time should be. However, wisdom and experience teach that perhaps it should be at least six months to a year after they meet the qualifications. Not six months to a year to *meet* the qualifications, but a proving time afterward to see if they are genuine. This time-frame will vary, but not greatly. It may take longer than a year with those who have moral and character deficiencies in their background.

The deacon qualifications of I Timothy 3:8-13 fall into three categories:

   A. **Character**
   B. **Domestic**
   C. **Spiritual**

There are also deacon qualifications listed in Acts chapter six which will be incorporated into these three categories. Some of the qualifications are the exact same ones for elders.

A. Character Qualifications

1. **A deacon is not to be double-tongued** (I Tim. 3:8). A deacon, at times, will be privy to personal information concerning members; he cannot be given to gossip. Being double-tongued means to say one thing to someone, and something different to someone else. A deacon must have his tongue under control (James 3:1-8). Other translations render this word as follows: "not shifty and double talkers but sincere in what they say"- Amplified Bible; "not false in word" - N.T. in Basic English; "straightforward men" - N. T. American Translation.

2. **A deacon is not to be given to wine** (I Tim. 3:8). This would include any form of intoxication. Wine was a common drink in Bible days; some was fermented, some unfermented. The fermented was less than 2% alcohol; it would have taken lots of it to get drunk. However, a deacon was still not to be given to it. The literal translation says "not tarrying at or staying near wine."

3. **A deacon is not to be greedy for money** (I Tim. 3:8). Money should never be the motivation for life's decisions. The love of money is a root of all sorts of evil (I Tim.6:10). The Greek word for "greedy for money" (*aischkrokerde*) means "not desirous of base gain; not using wrong methods to raise money to increase one's own income."

4. **A deacon is to be blameless** (I Tim. 3:10). A deacon's life is to be above reproach in all areas of life. A deacon is to be a godly example to the flock. The Greek word for "blameless" (anegkletos) means "to be unaccused." Other translations include: "if no objection is raised against them" - Twentieth Century N.T.; "if they are found irreproachable"- Conybeare; "if there is no. fault to be found with them" - N.T. American Translation; "if they are of unblemished character" – Weymouth.

5. **A deacon is to be proven** (I Tim. 3:10). The Greek word means "to be tested, examined and scrutinized to see whether a thing is genuine or not. It has the notion of proving a thing whether it be worthy to be received or not." The Weymouth translation renders it "probation." No deacon should be installed without a time of proving, regardless of educational or business background, and finances are of no consideration!

6. **A deacon is to be of a good reputation** (Acts 6:3). A deacon must have an excellent testimony and reputation with unbelievers and believers alike in the community. This includes areas of financial obligations; business dealings, community relations, legal matters, taxes, etc. In secular employment, it is important for a deacon to have the respect of his co-workers; he should not be slothful or critical of supervisors. A deacon is an example outside of the church as well as within. A deacon should also have a good report among the brethren. He should not have a history of leaving churches over

differences with the leadership. If this occurs it should be an exception, not a pattern.

B. Domestic Qualifications

1. **A deacon is to be the husband of one wife** (I Tim. 3:12). This qualification does not specifically involve divorce and/or remarriage though the two may relate. A deacon must be a loyal husband without adulterous relationships or attitudes. The Greek for this qualification is *mias gunaikos* meaning "of one woman." A literal translation would be "a one-woman husband." A deacon should be totally dedicated to his wife and not flirtatious. This qualification does not disqualify single men or women; the Apostle Paul himself was single. Other translations of this phrase include:

   - "Be appointed from those who have not been polygamous." N.T. according to Eastern Texts
   - "Faithful to his one wife." NEB

2. **A deacon is to rule his house well** (I Tim. 3:12). A deacon must preside over and manage the affairs of his household well. A deacon's house must be in order according to the Word of God (see I Cor. 11.3-12; Eph. 5.22- 32). The man is to be the head of the home. However, headship is not dictatorship. Headship involves concern and care and provision. The man is responsible for the overall direction of the family. A deacon must not guilty of heeding the voice of his wife above the voice of the Lord (Gen. 3:17).

3. **The deacon is to rule his children well** (I Tim. 3:12). Children are a reflection of the quality of home life.

Continuous upheaval in public is a sure sign that the home is not in order. The following guidelines for elder's children are applicable for deacon's children as well.

   a. A deacon's children should be in submission (I Tim. 3:4).
   b. A deacon's children should have reverence (I Tim. 3:4).
   c. A deacon's children should be faithful (Tit. 1:6).
   d. A deacon's children should not be accused of riot (Tit. 1:6).
   e. A deacon's children should not be insubordinate (Tit. 1:6).

4. **A deacon's wife is to meet certain qualifications** (I Tim. 3:11). Paul lists certain qualifications for the deacon's wives. These qualifications include:

   a. Reverent: This means "venerable, honorable, honest."
   b. Not Slanderous: Greek: *diabolis*, meaning "to give false report, injure another by defaming." This is the Greek word translated "Devil."
   c. Temperate: Self-control and discipline
   d. Faithful in all things: The deacon's wife should be reliable, trustworthy, and dependable.

C. Spiritual Qualifications

1. **A deacon is to be full of the Holy Spirit** (Acts 6:3). A requirement for deacons in the early church was that the candidate be baptized with the Holy Spirit. The baptism was no less than what the 120 received in the upper room (Acts 2:4); it was accompanied by the initial evidence of

speaking in other tongues. Today's candidates should meet the same requirements.

2. **A deacon is to be full of wisdom** (Acts 6:3). King Solomon, when granted any request that he desired from God, asked for and received wisdom. Wisdom is essential to any type of spiritual ministry. By acting unwisely, one can set back the move of God. Meditating in the book of Proverbs is helpful in making one wise.

3. **A deacon is to be reverent** (I Tim. 3:8). A deacon should possess a seriousness of mind and purpose in the things of God. There is a time to laugh and a time to be serious; a deacon must know the difference. A deacon should inspire reverence within others in the congregation. Other translations of this word "reverent" include:

   - "Worthy of respect" – Amplified Bible
   - "Dignified" – Emphasized N.T.
   - "Serious outlook" – Phillips
   - "High principle" – New English Bible

4. **A deacon is to hold the mystery of the faith with a pure conscience** (I Tim. 3:9). Deacons should be well taught in the Word. Many things will try to pull them from the simplicity of their faith, but they must hold fast. A deacon must keep a clean conscience before God, without such one will always be hindered.

   The New English Bible translates this verse this way: "These must be men who combine a clear conscience with a firm hold on the deep truths of our faith."

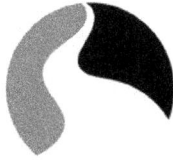

The Ministry of Deacons

The Origin of the Deaconate

As we learned in our word study, the first mention of the Greek word for deacon occurs before the book of Acts. It was used by Jesus, in a general sense for "servant." However, the origin of the official office of deacon does not occur until Acts chapter six. The office was born out of need.

> Acts 6:1-7
> **1 Now in those days, when the number of the disciples was multiplying, there arose a complaint against the Hebrews by the Hellenists, because their widows were neglected in the daily distribution.**
> **2 Then the twelve summoned the multitude of the disciples and said, "It is not desirable that we should leave the word of God and serve tables.**
> **3 Therefore, brethren, seek out from among you seven men of good reputation, full of the Holy Spirit and wisdom, whom we may appoint over this business;**
> **4 but we will give ourselves continually to prayer and to the ministry of the word."**
> **5 And the saying pleased the whole multitude. And they chose Stephen, a man full of faith and the Holy Spirit, and**

Philip, Prochorus, Nicanor, Timon, Parmenas, and Nicolas, a proselyte from Antioch,

6 whom they set before the apostles; and when they had prayed, they laid hands on them.

7 Then the word of God spread, and the number of the disciples multiplied greatly in Jerusalem, and a great many of the priests were obedient to the faith.

Division began to develop early on in the Church. Satan always wants to quench a revival with strife and division. In this case, the Greek speaking Jews, Hellenists, felt that they were being neglected in the daily distribution. At this point, the number of disciples was upward of eight thousand. The twelve were trying to oversee the whole operation of the Church. The physical needs of the people were beginning to overwhelm their ability to minister to the spiritual needs of the people, and more importantly, their ministry to the Lord.

The twelve finally gathered the whole multitude and said: "It is not desirable that we should leave the word of God and serve tables." The primary function of a pastor is the ministry of the Word of God. Many times, congregations want to wear down a pastor with endless menial tasks that deprive the pastor from receiving a fresh Word from God. Satan loves to have it so. God's people go hungry, and the devil destroys them due to their lack of knowledge (Hos. 4:6). Every pastor should take a stand and say with the twelve: "We will give ourselves continually to prayer and to the ministry of the word"

God gave the twelve wisdom to delegate the physical responsibilities to capable men within the congregation. Seven deacons were selected upon meeting the apostle's requirements. These deacons were "over this business" of ministering to the physical needs of the congregation. This immediately freed up the apostles to spend time with God in prayer and the Word. The anointing of God increased upon them as a result. The effect upon the congregation was no less dynamic:

Acts 6:7 And the word of God spread, and the number of the disciples multiplied greatly in Jerusalem

Deacon Boards?

Many modem churches are governed by so-called "deacon boards." The deacons form a committee and vote on the decisions of the church. Their authority far out ranks the office of pastor. They have the right to hire and fire pastors unilaterally. The pastor is more-less a hired employee of these deacons, and is under their authority at all times.

This is a ludicrous setup from a Biblical standpoint! Nowhere in the Word of God is such a system carried out. One can in no way arrive at this type of authority from analyzing the function of the original seven. Theirs was a job of serving tables (Acts 6:2)! The operation of deacon boards is false church government. The deaconate is strictly a ministry of helps, not a governmental, decision making position.

Old Testament Levites

New Testament deacons were preceded in type by the Old Testament Levites. The tribe of Levi was chosen to be the "servant tribe." They assisted the priesthood in the ministry of helps. Their duties consisted of the following:

- Service to the Lord.
- Service in the Tabernacle: transporting it, as well as serving in the worship aspects.

- Service to the priests. Priestly functions were spiritual; Levite duties were primarily physical service. Without the Levites, the priests could not properly function.
- Service of the sacrifices; altar service.
- Service to the 12 tribes; service to widows, orphans, etc.
- Service in the Law of God.

Service of their New Testament counterparts, deacons, is somewhat similar, yet uniquely distinct.

The Deacon's Job Description

In this section, I will list the many ministries and functions of a deacon. No one should be given a job without a thorough job description. One cannot be held accountable to do what one does not know to do. This is a major cause of frustration among church leaders: "What exactly is my job?"

As with the elder's list, the following deacon's list is not exhaustive, but thorough. Some churches may have no need for certain ministries listed; some may have additional ministry needs not listed here. Each church should personally adapt a job description for the deacon's ministry.

This list is not necessarily given in the order of importance. Importance is determined by the needs; needs vary from church to church. The needs of the early church foremost involved the daily distribution of material supplies. This may not be a pressing need in some churches, though all should have a ministry to the poor. Though some Scripture references will be given, the Bible does not enumerate every function of a deacon. Deacons primarily meet practical needs; therefore, many of the duties listed are observations of practical needs in the every-day life of a church.

The Ministry of Care to the Poor: This need for ministry to the poor is what gave birth to the office of deacon in the early church (Acts 6). Jesus said that when it is done to the least of the brethren, it is done unto Him (Matt. 25:40). Jesus outlined five areas of practical ministry in Matthew 25. Three of the five dealt with ministry to the poor:

1. Food for the hungry and thirsty
2. Shelter for the stranger
3. Clothing for the naked

The Ministry of Care to Widows and Orphans: This ministry involves both spiritual and physical care. The early church made a practice of relieving true widows and visiting the orphans. It is a deacon's responsibility to take the lead in this type of ministry (as can be seen in Acts chapter six).

I Timothy 5:3-16 gives detailed instructions on the handling of the widow's ministry. James 1:27 says: "Pure and undefiled religion before God and the Father is this: to visit orphans and widows in their trouble, and to keep oneself unspotted from the world"

The Ministry of Follow-Up to Absentees: Hebrews 10:25   stresses the importance of assembling together as a body, or community of faith – the family of God. Deacons should be involved in follow-up ministry to absentees. Each week that goes by for an absentee makes it harder for them to get back in the habit of attending church.

Deacons should be assigned a designated group of families to follow up on if and when absent. These contacts should be made within 48 hours, either in person or by phone. Written reports should be handed in to the church office.

The Ministry of Soul-winning and Discipleship: Evangelism is a commandment for all who are followers of Jesus Christ (Matt. 28:18-19; Mark 16:15-20). Deacons, especially, need to set a standard of excellence in soul-winning. Theirs is not only a physical service, but spiritual as well.

Philip was one of the original seven deacons appointed by the apostles (Acts 6:5). Upon the scattering of the Church (Acts 8:4), Philip went down to Samaria to preach the gospel. Acts 8:5 says, "Then Philip went down to the city of Samaria and preached Christ to them." Philip was also used in mighty signs and wonders, proving that the deaconate is to be a supernatural ministry. Later in life, Philip was referred to as an evangelist (Acts 21:8); the only one so-named in the New Testament.

The Ministry of Personal Assistance to the Pastors: The office of the deacon was originally brought about to relieve the physical duties that the apostles were performing (Acts 6:1-4). This type of assistance is of great value to the pastoral staff. There are many "little things" that need to be done in a ministry. If the pastor has to do all of "little things" there will be very little time left for the spiritual things.

In Paul's ministry, there seems to be quite a few men and women who served him personally in the capacity of a deacon, or minister of helps. Here are a few:

- John Mark (Acts 13:5; II Tim. 4:11)
- Tychicus (Col. 4:7)
- Timothy (Acts 19:21-22)
- Erastus (Acts 19:21-22)
- Onesiphoros (II Tim. 1:16-18)
- Phebe (Rom. 16:1-2)

- Luke (II Tim. 4:11)

The Ministry of Errands: The root word for "deacon" is *diako* and it literally means "to run or to hasten on errands." There are many errands that need to be run in the ministry. They can be time consuming and at times exhausting. The deacon's ministry is invaluable in this department.

The Ministry of Assistance to Guest Speakers: The life of an itinerant minister can be very difficult. All do not travel with an entourage of helpers and assistants. This is the exception rather than the norm. Most traveling ministers are solely dependent upon the hospitality of the host church. Hospitality is a gift that deacons must demonstrate.

The early church was instructed on how to receive guest ministers:

> **III John 1:**
> **5 Beloved, you do faithfully whatever you do for the brethren and for strangers,**
> **6 who have borne witness of your love before the church. If you send them forward on their journey in a manner worthy of God, you will do well,**
> **7 because they went forth for His name's sake, taking nothing from the Gentiles.**
> **8 We therefore ought to receive such, that we may become fellow workers for the truth.**

Some of the things that need to be done for a guest speaker include:

a) Making reservations at the hotel
b) Transportation from the airport if flying
c) Making sure that the meals of the guest are taken care of
d) Transportation to and from the services

e) Personal assistance during the services, as well as before and after

f) Protecting the guest from draining individuals

The Ministry of Ushering: Ushering takes on quite an important role in a public worship service. When sufficient ushering is not provided, chaos can develop. Deacons are good candidates for ushering.

Organization is the key to successful ushering. It is important to know the following:

- Who is in charge
- Who is ushering each service
- Who works which aisle
- What is to be done with the offering after the collection
- Who counts the offering
- What to do if someone is disruptive
- The location of all areas of the church facility (e.g., nursery, restrooms)

The Ministry of Prayer Line Help: When the minister calls people forward for prayer, it is important that there be organization so that no one gets overlooked. There are also times when someone being prayed for will fall out under the Spirit. Someone needs to be there to assist them. Even if someone falls out in the flesh, it is important to make sure they don't injure themselves.

Those assisting in this area need to remain prayerful during the entire time. Any demonstration of the flesh can hinder the anointing of God from ministering into people's lives.

The Ministry of Keeping Order in the Services: Disruptions are the work of Satan to steal the Word of God from people's hearts. A deacon should be polite, but at the same time, not allow a disturbance to continue. Constant moving about and people going in and out of the sanctuary can grieve the Spirit of God. The House of God is a place of reverence. Children should not be permitted to run wild. God does not bless a spirit of unruliness.

The Ministry of Children's Church: The children's ministry of a local church will be one of the key determining factors on whether a family returns after visiting the church. Some deacons and deaconesses are called to children's ministry. This is truly a high and heavenly calling!

The Ministry of Serving Communion: As well as being a function of elders, deacons are to assist in serving communion in the House of the Lord. A deacon should carefully study I Corinthians 11:23-32. If communion is to be received in a worthy manner, it must also be served with reverence.

In both receiving and serving communion, it is imperative that there be no unconfessed sin or unforgiveness in the heart. Deacons must keep their hearts pure of the defilement of bitterness and resentment.

The Ministry of Baptizing: Jesus not only gave the commandment to preach the gospel, but to baptize those who believe (Matt. 28:19). Whenever possible, baptism should be done publically by church leadership. Philip was a deacon and he baptized the Ethiopian eunuch (Acts 8:38). Baptism serves as identification with the death, burial and resurrection of our Lord. It also serves as identification with His body; this is why it is best done by church leaders.

Baptism should be done "in the name of the Father and of the Son and of the Holy Spirit" (Matt. 28:19). "In the authority of the name of Jesus" may also be added according to Acts 2:39. Instructions on how to baptize are listed in the Elder's section.

The Ministry of Record Keeping: Certain records are to be kept by deacons. These records include:

- Offering totals
- Sunday school attendance
- Worship attendance
- Follow-up results

Record keeping doesn't seem too spiritual, but someone has to do it. How else would we know how many were in the upper room on the day of Pentecost (120), or how many were saved that day (3,000)?
In the Old Testament, "recorders" are mentioned several times. These recorders would copy down any prophecy that was given by the man of God. Some of the Psalms are a by-product of this ministry.

The Ministry of Administrative Work: A church secretary is a ministry of helps. Many times, the secretary is the first contact a person has with the church when a call or visit to the office is made. A deacon or deaconess may serve in this capacity. Many pastors could not begin to function in an organized manner without an administrative assistant. If one's church cannot afford to hire a secretary, deacons should volunteer their services part-time in any of a number of areas: phone answering, computer work, letter writing, filing, etc.

The Ministry of the Gifts of the Spirit: I Corinthians 12:8-10 lists off nine gifts or manifestations of the Spirit: word of wisdom, word of knowledge, Faith, gifts of healings, working of miracles, prophecy, discerning of spirits, different kinds of tongues and interpretation of tongues.

These gifts are available to all believers, as verse seven says, "But the manifestation of the Spirit is given to each one for the profit of all." Deacons are called upon to minister to people continually. Philip is a classic example of a deacon that operated in the gifts of the Spirit (Acts 8:6). Deacons should earnestly desire the gifts, and operate them in love (I Cor. 12:31).

The Ministry of Deliverance: When Jesus sent out the twelve disciples He gave them power over unclean spirits (Matt. 10:1). Demons will oppose the going forth of the gospel. The first sign that Jesus said would follow a believer when they went out to preach the gospel was casting out demons (Mark 16:15-17).

Deacons must be spiritually prepared to minister to the oppressed and possessed. As a deacon, Philip cast out devils while in Samaria: "For unclean spirits, crying with a loud voice, came out of many who were possessed" (Acts 8:7).

The Ministry of Building and Property Maintenance: There is an extremely large amount of maintenance care that needs to be done, even in a small church. Someone needs to clean the church building (no one wants to come to a dirty church building). Someone needs to cut the grass (or hire some goats to graze). At different times, the roof needs repaired, the parking lot graveled, or the building painted.

All of this can be hired done, but this is something many churches cannot afford. The deacon's ministry should come to the rescue in these cases. And one person should not be doing all the work just because they will. Volunteers from the congregation should be sought regularly.

The Ministry of a Parking Attendant: Entering the church premises is the first impression one has of your church; leaving those same premises is the last impression. Needless to say, it should be a convenient, if not pleasant, experience. Is it not true that one of the greatest battles for the fruit of the Spirit in our lives can take place behind the wheel of a car? A helpful attendant can make sure that none of those frustrating moments take place on the parking lot of the church. Assistance also needs to be given to the elderly and handicapped.

These and other helps ministries are valuable to the ongoing success of the church. According to each individual church, some will be more prominent than others. Some have escaped the list entirely. The lead pastor should develop a personalized job description for the deacon's ministry that best suits his church. The deacon's role is a ministry of helps; any area of the church that needs help is a potential ministry for a deacon.

Appointment and Terms of Deacons

It is important to understand how one enters the office of a deacon, and how one is to leave that same office if the situation arises. As can be seen from the Acts chapter six passage, the congregation took a part in the selection of the original seven.

Acts 6:3 Therefore, brethren, seek out from among you seven men of good reputation, full of the Holy Spirit and wisdom, whom we may appoint over this business

At this time, the congregation was so large (eight thousand plus) that it was impractical for the twelve to find seven men from the multitude. Therefore, the responsibility was delegated to certain brethren. However, it can be clearly seen that certain qualifications, prescribed by the apostles, had to be met. Also, the apostles were the ones that did the actual appointing. It was their prerogative to reject any candidate brought forth.

This same method of appointment may be followed today, with minor variations, in larger congregations. However, in smaller ones the need for delegation in this process may be eliminated. This is not to say that the deacons selected should not have the congregation's general approval. Whether the church is large or small, whether delegation in the selection process is used or not, the final decision rests with the lead pastor.

The term of a deacon is indefinite unless certain conditions develop. These conditions may include:

- Sin in the deacon's life
- Unfaithfulness to the church
- Insubordination to the church leadership
- A deacon's lack of desire to continue in the office

Other situations may also occur which necessitate the removal of a deacon, such as moving from the area. At all times, it is the pastor's prerogative to appoint or dismiss a deacon for legitimate reasons. An important spiritual principle remains: he who has the authority to appoint you has the authority to remove you.

What About Women?

Consider the following partial list of women that were used by God in the Bible:

1. **Miriam** was a prophetess and one of only three spiritual leaders over the nation of Israel, along with Moses and Aaron. (Exodus 15:20)
2. **Deborah** was a judge, a prophetess and a mother of Israel for over 40 years. (Judges 4:4).
3. **Huldah** was a prophetess (II Chron. 34:22-28).
4. **The woman of Samaria** was used by God to preach the Gospel to an entire city (John 4:39-42).
5. **Mary Magdalene** was the first to preach His resurrection (John 20:17-18). Saint Augustine wrote that she was, :The first preacher of the resurrection of Christ
6. **Philip's four daughters** were prophetesses (Acts 21:8.10).
7. **Priscilla** was a teacher and pastor along with her husband Aquila. Her ministry was received by the apostle Apollos (Acts 18:24-28).

Romans chapter 16 gives us the clearest evidence of women in ministry roles in the early church. In this chapter alone Paul mentions ten women who were fellow-workers with him in the Gospel. Most notably, in the first seven verses he lists a female deacon, a husband and wife pastoral team, and a husband and wife apostolic team.

A Female Deacon:
I commend unto you Phebe our sister, which is a servant [Greek: DEACON] of the church which is at Cenchrea (v. 1).

A Female Pastor:
Greet Priscilla and Aquila my helpers in Christ Jesus... Likewise greet the church that is in their house (vv. 3, 5).

A Female Apostle:
Salute Andronicus and Junia, my kinsmen and my fellowprisoners, who are of note among the apostles (v 7).

While Bible revelation is clear that the majority of church leadership should be male, there is Biblical precedent for women in leadership as long as they are submitted to authority. Women in the early church served in apostolic, prophetic, evangelistic, pastoral, and teaching ministries. The offices of elder and deacon are beneath these. The five-fold offices are the ones who set the elders and deacons in (Acts 6:6, 14:23, Titus 1:5).

The one who appoints you is over you in the Lord. If it is scriptural for women to serve in these higher offices, it is without question acceptable to serve beneath them. An apostle is the highest rank of church government and Junia had this office (Rom.16:7)

As has already, been laid out, there are different levels of elders in the Word of God. All five-fold ministers are elders, but not all elders are five-fold ministers. The very fact that all five-fold ministers are elders, and women are qualified to be five-fold ministers, qualifies women to be elders. Women deacons are named as such in the Word of God (Rom. 16:1).

What about the qualifications given in I Timothy 3:14? Aren't these for men only? One of the qualifications is ruling well their own house (v 4). Paul is writing to address the most common scenario. Otherwise single men would be excluded from this office as well, for it says they must be the husband of one wife (v 2). This itself would eliminate Paul. No, Paul is giving guidelines for the norm, that being a married man. This should still be the norm today, but that does not eliminate the exception, a single man or a qualified woman.

Paul calls Phebe a deacon in Romans 16:1. He goes on to give instructions regarding her ministry in verse two:

> **Romans 16:2 That you may receive her in the Lord in a manner worthy of the saints, and assist her in whatever business she has need of you; for indeed she has been a helper of many and of myself also.**

Paul tells the church to *receive* her. "Receive" is also translated "accept" and "allow" in the New Testament. Don't just put up with her, but genuinely receive her from your heart! Draw from her ministry without respect to gender.

He also says to assist her. She was in charge of certain business in the church and Paul said to assist her. Do whatever she tells you to help get the job done. If God can use mule tell a prophet what to do, then He can use a woman. Some won't take instructions from a woman; they are too prideful. If you were dying and the only doctor available was a woman, would you let her be in charge? Of course! Her authority is based on her knowledge. If a woman knows how to do the job better – assist her.

Paul said she had been a "succorer" of many." The original Greek word for "succorer" is the feminine derivative of "prostemi" which is translated "rule" five times including in I Timothy 3:4, 5, and 12. It is translated "over" in I Thes. 5:12. Paul said there have been times when even he placed himself under her direction.

127

In Paul's letter to Titus he tells him to set things in order and to ordain elders (Titus 1:5). "Elders" is the word "presbutero;" this word speaks of spiritual maturity. In chapter two of Titus it speaks of the "aged women." Now was Paul talking simply about physically old women or is there another meaning? The word for "aged women" is the same root word for "elders" in 1:5. The translators were interpreting, rather than giving a uniform rendering. It could correctly be translated "women elders." Choosing different English words for the same Greek word is always an interpretation based on context. Let's look at the passage, and you decide for yourself.

> **Titus 2:**
> **3 the older women likewise, that they be reverent in behavior, not slanderers, not given to much wine, teachers of good things—**
> **4 that they admonish the young women to love their husbands, to love their children,**
> **5 to be discreet, chaste, homemakers, good, obedient to their own husbands, that the word of God may not be blasphemed.**

The text gives many of the same qualifications listed in I Timothy 3 and Titus 1 for elders. Paul lists things such as holiness, not false accusers, not given to wine, and teachers of good things (v 3). These are matters of spiritual maturity.

Paul goes on in verses four and five and gives domestic qualifications. They are to love and obey their husbands and love their children. They are to be discreet and an example to other ladies.

Based on the fact that "aged" is the same Greek word for "elder," and it is used in the same context as when rendered "elder," I believe it is referring to the same spiritual ministry, whether titled such or not. Elder is a function not a title. Remember Paul's emphasis in the letter is ordaining elders and setting things in order.

Study Questions, Part 3

1. What was Paul's purpose in leaving Titus in Crete?

_____

_____

_____

2. What three men in the New Testament are referred to as pillars?

_____

3. What counsel was given to Moses to help him from "burning out"? What were the two occasions where this counsel was given? Who were the two that gave the counsel?

_____

_____

_____

_____

4. Describe the "Jethro Principle."

_____

_____

5. What was Moses' job description? What were the elders' job descriptions?

Moses:

_____

_____

Elders:

_____

_____

6. An individual should use his/her _____ to build the church, not use he _____ to build his/her ministry.

7. The terms "Elder" and "Deacon" are primarily _____, rather than _____.

8. What is the key difference between the terms "elder" and "bishop"?

Elder:

_____

Bishop:

_____

9. Define a presbytery.

_____

_____

10. What are the three categories of qualifications for elders?

_____

_____

11. What does Paul mean when he says: "The husband of one wife"?

_____

_____

_____

12. Under what circumstances should the actions of a family member disqualify a candidate?

_____

_____

_____

13. Is calling and anointing sufficient grounds for setting apart an elder? Why?

_____

_____

_____

14. What are the three phases involved in an individual being put in as an elder?

_____

_____

15. What is the primary way one can tell if someone is called to a specific spiritual work?

_____

_____

16. What is the wrong approach to appointing elders?

_____

_____

17. What is the correct method of appointing elders?

_____

_____

18. Whose representatives (extensions) are the elders? Why?

_____

_____

_____

19. Describe the transference that took place between Moses and the seventy elders.

_____

_____

_____

20. Why is it important for elders to have the same philosophy of ministry as the pastors?

_____

_____

21. What is the difference between vision of ministry and philosophy of ministry?

_____

_____

_____

22. Where there is a difference of _____ , there will eventually be a difference of _____ .

23. Who does the vision and philosophy of ministry begin with? Why?

_____

_____

_____

24. The purpose of elders is not to _____ the leadership of the pastors, but to _____ it.

25. Name three Old Testament leaders that had elders (Give Scripture references).

    1. _____

    2. _____

    3. _____

26. The New Testament gives a _____ _____ of church government.

27. Each church should personally adapt a _____ for the elder's ministry.

28. What factor determines the importance of a particular ministry?

_____

_____

29. How many reasons does the New Testament give for excommunicating a member? Which four involve trouble making and strife?

_____

_____

_____

30. What is the goal of excommunication, or any type of correction?

_____

_____

31. What three steps of restoration did Paul instruct the Corinthian church to make toward their sinning member after he repented?

    1. _____

    2. _____

    3. _____

32. What is an elder's responsibility towards those who are rebellious toward leadership?

_____

_____

33. Who has the final say in the decision-making process? How should the elders respond to that decision?

_____

_____

34. What extra measures should elders take with new converts in the congregation?

_____

_____

35. What trap must elders avoid in the area of counseling? What should the elder do once this trap has been identified?

_____

_____

36. How should private counseling with the opposite sex be handled?

_____

_____

_____

37. The elders remain under the supervision of the _____ at all times.

38. An elder that is not prepared to confront _____ should not be an elder.

39. Those with the genuine ministry of _____ have no strings attached!

40. The success of Paul's early ministry hinged largely on one man's obedience, and another's encouragement. Who were those men, and how did they affect Paul's ministry?

_____

_____

_____

41. What five ways are listed with which an elder may encourage the pastors?

   1. _____

   2. _____

   3. _____

   4. _____

   5. _____

42. Can you think of any jobs that an elder should perform which are not listed? If so, what are they?

_____

_____

_____

43. Combining all three Greek words for *deacon*, give a good definition of the term.

_____

_____

44. What qualifications are a deacon's wife required to meet?

_____

_____

_____

45. Describe the circumstance from which the office of a deacon was born.

_____

_____

_____

46. Why are deacon boards a false church government?

_____

_____

_____

47. What role did the apostles play in the appointment of deacons? What role did the congregation play? How might these roles vary according to the circumstances?

_____

_____

_____

_____

48. The term of a deacon is indefinite unless certain circumstances develop; what are some of those conditions?

_____

_____

_____

49. Who is the female deacon listed in Romans chapter 16?

_____

50. Explain why Titus chapter two refers to female elders and not elderly women.

_____

_____

_____

_____

_____

Section Four: A Pastor's Guide to the Pasture

Shepherding and Feeding the Sheep

The New Testament ministry of an elder, both five-fold and supportive, is primarily a shepherding ministry. In John 21:15-17, Jesus told Simon Peter three times that if he loved Him, to feed and tend His sheep.

> **John 21:**
>
> **15 So when they had eaten breakfast, Jesus said to Simon Peter, "Simon, son of Jonah, do you love Me more than these?"**
>
> **He said to Him, "Yes, Lord; You know that I love You."**
>
> **He said to him, "Feed My lambs."**
>
> **16 He said to him again a second time, "Simon, son of Jonah, do you love Me?"**
>
> **He said to Him, "Yes, Lord; You know that I love You."**
>
> **He said to him, "Tend My sheep."**
>
> **17 He said to him the third time, "Simon, son of Jonah, do you love Me?" Peter was grieved because He said to him the third time, "Do you love Me?"**
>
> **And he said to Him, "Lord, You know all things; You know that I love You."**
>
> **Jesus said to him, "Feed My sheep."**

In this passage there are two different words used for "feed." The first one is "bosko" (vv. 15, 17). Bosko means "to feed, nourish, provide food." This speaks of the need for teaching the Word of God.

The pastor's (shepherd's) primary role is to feed the sheep. The authority to lead is predicated on the ability to feed. If no one is feeding then no one is leading. Five-fold elders, not supportive elders, perform this function.

The second word is "poimaino" (v. 16). Poimaino means "to tend, to watch over, to care for." While bosko is the primary task of five-fold elders, poimaino is secondary, though just as important (see Acts 6:4). Poimaino is the primary function of supportive elders. There needs to be in each local church a team of supportive elders that tend to, watch over and care for the sheep. This is not to say that a pastor shouldn't carry out this function also, but there's only so much that one or two pastors can accomplish. Poimaino shepherding is the primary ministry of supportive elders. Their function is not to tell the shepherd/pastor how to do his job. Their role in the pasture is that of a sheepdog.

To carry out this "poimaino ministry" it is imperative for elders, both five-fold and supportive, to have a solid understanding of the pasture. A knowledge of sheep is required, but also knowledge of goats and wolves as well.

The following is a general description of sheep, goats, wolves and sheepdogs.

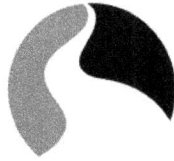

Sheep

When God refers to His people as sheep, it is not *necessarily* a compliment. Though there are many fine qualities about a sheep, it is perhaps best to begin with the negative characteristics:

a. Sheep have no defense system to protect themselves; no sharp teeth or claws.
b. Sheep have no sense of direction; they cannot find their way home if lost.
c. If sheep fall on their backs, they cannot turn themselves upright.
d. Sheep by nature are easily given to rivalry and competition.

There are also many positive qualities about sheep. Though they seem so weak and helpless, this only causes a deep reliance to develop towards the shepherd. Self-reliance is a drawback to working in God's kingdom. God needs submissive, obedient sheep that will follow Him.

The twenty-third Psalm reveals several wonderful qualities about spiritual sheep:

Psalm 23
23 The Lord is my shepherd; I shall not want.
2 He makes me to lie down in green pastures; He leads me beside the still waters.

3 He restores my soul; He leads me in the paths of righteousness for His name's sake.

4 Yea, though I walk through the valley of the shadow of death, I will fear no evil; for You are with me; Your rod and Your staff, they comfort me.

5 You prepare a table before me in the presence of my enemies; You anoint my head with oil; my cup runs over.

6 Surely goodness and mercy shall follow me

All the days of my life; and I will dwell[a] in the house of the Lord forever.

From this magnificent psalm, we can glean the following:

a. Sheep trust God to meet their needs: spiritually, mentally, emotionally, physically, and financially (v. 1)

b. Sheep like to lie down in green pastures (v. 2). Green pastures represent God's Word. Sheep love to be fed the true Word of God.

c. True sheep are led by the Spirit (e.g., "He leads me" v. 2). There is longevity and quality to their decisions.

d. God's sheep love still waters (v. 2), not troubled or agitated waters, but still waters. Spiritual sheep shun dissention and strife.

e. Sheep love a righteous standard (e.g., "paths of righteousness" v. 3b). Sheep love the truth, even when it hurts. Goats call it legalism.

f. Sheep respond positively to the rod (correction) and staff (protection) (v. 4).

g. Sheep stay in the fold in the presence of enemies (v. 5). Troubles and attacks won't drive them away from the church.

h. Sheep constantly need fresh oil (v. 5b). They want the anointing of God; sheep won't settle for less.

i. True sheep display contentment for the house (singular) of God (v. 6). There is no compulsion to roam (church hop).

j. Goodness and mercy follow sheep (v. 6b), not the other way around.

In summary, sheep need a lot of care and attention. But their desire is to be faithful, loyal and submissive. They are a joy to the shepherd, as the writer to the Hebrews expressed:

Hebrews 13:17
Obey those who rule over you, and be submissive, for they watch out for your souls, as those who must give account. Let them do so with joy and not with grief, for that would be unprofitable for you.

Next, we will look at goats.

Goats

Jesus discussed the opposite characteristics of sheep and goats in Matthew chapter 25 in the context of the final judgment. We will not base our review of goats in this same context, as only Jesus is qualified to make the final judgment, and that on the last day. However, Jesus does make a point that is relevant to our discussion in verse 32: "a shepherd divides his sheep from the goats."

> **Matthew 25:**
> **31 "When the Son of Man comes in His glory, and all the holy angels with Him, then He will sit on the throne of His glory.**
> **32 All the nations will be gathered before Him, and He will separate them one from another, as a shepherd divides his sheep from the goats.**
> **33 And He will set the sheep on His right hand, but the goats on the left.**

Within the church, it is not so much a physical separation, but a spiritual one. A good shepherd will know his sheep from his goats and pastor them accordingly. For along with sheep, goats are part of every shepherd's fold. As mentioned, goats display many of the opposite characteristics of sheep:

a. Sheep like to be led; Goats like to roam. They have the "grass is greener somewhere else" syndrome.

b. Sheep like still waters; Goats thrive in turmoil and strife.

c. Sheep are easily corrected; Goats are stubborn or "butting" in nature.

d. Sheep like to get along; Goats are always agitating others with their words and ways.

e. Sheep like to lie in rest, trusting their shepherds; Goats are always suspicious of their leaders. Goats profess to have the "gift of discernment." What they have is the "gift" of suspicion.

In summary, goats are not easy to pastor, but they still need a shepherd. Their threat is to the pasture, not the flock itself, as they are not carnivorous. A goat can change its ways and become sheepish. However, the biggest hindrance to this occurring is the goat's propensity to roam. Goats won't stay anywhere long enough to let the Word change them. When something on the "menu" is to their personal distaste, they're off again to another pasture.

Going back to the message of Jesus in Matthew chapter 25, we can draw one other conclusion about the nature of goats: they like to talk the talk, but not walk the walk. They will be there for all that brings recognition in the eyes of man, but when true ministry in the trenches is being done, they are elsewhere.

Matthew 25:
44 "Then they also will answer Him, saying, 'Lord, when did we see You hungry or thirsty or a stranger or naked or sick or in prison, and did not minister to You?'
45 Then He will answer them, saying, 'Assuredly, I say to you, inasmuch as you did not do it to one of the least of these, you did not do it to Me.'

One word of caution to pastors: Jesus said to leave the ninety-nine sheep to go search for the one lost *sheep*. You don't leave the sheep to go retrieve the goat. They are roamers; while they were there you did as much as you could with them; now they are gone. They will be in a new sheepfold next Sunday, saying the same wonderful things about their new church that they use to say about yours.

> **Luke 15:**
> **4 "What man of you, having a hundred sheep, if he loses one of them, does not leave the ninety-nine in the wilderness, and go after the one which is lost until he finds it?**
> **5 And when he has found it, he lays it on his shoulders, rejoicing.**
> **6 And when he comes home, he calls together his friends and neighbors, saying to them, 'Rejoice with me, for I have found my sheep which was lost!'**

One sign that a pastor has lost his spiritual sight is the heavy reliance upon goats within his circle of influence. Goats often have financial resources or musical talents that can be used to manipulate leadership. When the power play comes, i.e., "I'm pulling out if I don't get my way," and the pastor compromises, it is an open door for sin and chaos to run rampant within the flock.

Our study next takes us to wolves.

Wolves

Unlike sheep and goats, wolves are carnivorous, flesh-eating animals. They don't feed on the pasture, but on the flock. Jesus said that they would often come disguised in sheep's clothing.

> **Matthew 7:15**
> **Beware of false prophets, who come to you in sheep's clothing, but inwardly they are ravenous wolves.**

Every pastor and elder needs discernment against the operation of wolves. The Apostle Paul warned the elders of Ephesus about wolves in his farewell speech to them:

> **Acts 20:29-30**
> **For I know this, that after my departure savage wolves will come in among you, not sparing the flock. Also from among yourselves, men will rise up, speaking perverse things, to draw away the disciples after themselves**

The sole desire of wolves is to devour the flock. Notice that Paul said "after my departure." Wolves know when the pastors are in authority and when they're not. Wolves aren't looking for a fight; they're looking for easy prey. Also notice that Paul warned that men would rise up among them and display wolfish characteristics. Pastors need an early detection system to alert them when this type of rebellion is occurring. This early detection system is the Holy Spirit, coupled with elders/sheepdogs who walk in the Spirit.

An isolated, solitaire sheep will easily be devoured; he is no match for a wolf. As mentioned, sheep have no defense system to fight off enemy attacks. The only defense a sheep has against a wolf is to stay in the fold, and stay submitted to the shepherd. When a wolf enters a sheepfold, sheep will press up tight against one another. The wolf will jump up on top of the sheep and pounce up and down, trying to separate them. Individually, the wolf will devour them. If the sheep stay in unity, the wolf has no penetration. It is imperative for sheep to stay in the fold!

It is also important that sheep be in a fold where there are true shepherds, not hirelings. Jesus warned us that the hireling will see the wolf coming and flee for his own safety, leaving the sheep as open prey.

> **John 10:11-13**
> **11 "I am the good shepherd. The good shepherd gives His life for the sheep. 12 But a hireling, he who is not the shepherd, one who does not own the sheep, sees the wolf coming and leaves the sheep and flees; and the wolf catches the sheep and scatters them. 13 The hireling flees because he is a hireling and does not care about the sheep.**

A shepherd will lay down his life for the sheep. Elders must also fall into this category. This was the emphasis of what Paul was saying to the Ephesian elders.

The following are some of the traits of wolves:

a. Wolves, run in packs, but have little respect for one another and will easily turn against one another.

148

b. Wolves do their best to stay away from the shepherds and cling to the sheep. However, the ones in sheep's clothing often try to seduce the pastors.

c. Wolves are easily exposed when flesh and carnality crop up. They will be all over it.

d. Wolves have problems with church leadership wherever they go. They have common denominators of being "hurt" by their previous pastors and "not having their gift received" in their last church. Beware!

e. Wolves often display a deceptive charismatic charm.

f. Wolves are sent by the devil to steal, kill and destroy (John 10:10). They are Satan's agents of destruction.

As seen in Acts 20:30, some people can turn wolfish without being properly submitted to the pastors. They will "draw away" other members of the congregation with their deceit. The chief aim of a wolf is to draw sheep away from the flock which God placed them. They will speak smooth words of how the pastors have "hurt" them, or how the Holy Spirit has "shown them" that the pastors are in error. This is designed to inject distrust for the leadership and instill confusion about where they're supposed to be.

In summary, wolves must be kept out of the flock at all costs! There are no exceptions. Compromising to entertain a wolf will always result in the loss of one or more sheep.

Part of the protection against wolves in the sheepfold is the ministry of sheepdogs. That will be our next discussion

Sheepdogs

Sheepdogs are an aid to the shepherd in keeping the sheep *in* and keeping the wolves *out*. The shepherd cannot be everywhere at the same time. Wolves are looking for vulnerable areas, places of weakness. As mentioned, wolves are not looking for a fight, but easy prey. Sheepdogs keep the sheep from being easy prey. While the shepherd is leading the flock (the role of pastors), sheepdogs stay along the perimeters of the fold to keep the sheep *in* and the wolves *out*.

What are some of the functions of a sheepdog?

a. Sheepdogs warn and protect the sheep of danger by barking or even a nip on the leg. Sheepdogs must be able to lovingly correct the sheep.

b. Sheepdogs will square off against a wolf to preserve the well-being of the sheepfold. Confrontation is part of their function.

c. Sheepdogs will inform the shepherds of problems and potential problems. Shepherds cannot be everywhere at the same time. Sheepdogs are on more of a peer level with the sheep and consequently see problems in the root stage. Often, pastors don't see the problem until it has come to fruition, which sometimes is too late to correct.

What are some of the qualities one needs to be a good sheepdog?

a. A consistent prayer life.
b. Spiritual discernment
c. A love for the sheep.
d. Loyalty to the pastors.
e. A disdain for the flesh/carnality.

In summary, sheepdogs are invaluable to the well-being of the flock. They provide the *poimaino* type of shepherding that is necessary for the fold to grow.

One caution: Sheepdogs are carnivorous, but they don't eat sheep; they eat meat prepared from the shepherd's hand. If for some reason a sheepdog gets a taste for the sheep, he must be removed. Church splits often occur through a sheepdog's disloyalty. It is a shepherd's responsibility to monitor the activities of the sheepdogs. If a sheepdog regularly doesn't show up to be fed by the shepherd (submission), there's a good chance that it is dipping into the sheep. However, if properly trained and monitored, a sheepdog is the shepherd's best friend.

The Vertical Pastor

The purpose for this book is to equip local churches to reach their fullest potential and usher in the glory of God. For this to happen, the man of God needs to spend time in God's presence. A recent survey was completed by interviewing the top 100 church planters in the world. The objective was to find a common denominator on their success with building churches. At the end of the survey there was only one common denominator among the 100 pastors. They all used different types of worship, had different preaching styles, used different types of facilities, etc. But one thing they all had in common... all 100. Each of them prayed two to three hours a day. There is great power in spending time with God.

Do you remember the story of when Jesus visited with Martha and Mary? The two sisters had very different approaches to ministry or service. Martha was very hands-on and assertive. Whatever needed done, she was there to make it happen. On the other hand, Mary was content to sit at the Master's feet and hear His Word.

> **Luke 10:**
> **38 Now it happened as they went that He entered a certain village; and a certain woman named Martha welcomed Him into her house.**

39 And she had a sister called Mary, who also sat at Jesus' feet and heard His word.

40 But Martha was distracted with much serving, and she approached Him and said, "Lord, do You not care that my sister has left me to serve alone? Therefore tell her to help me."

41 And Jesus answered and said to her, "Martha, Martha, you are worried and troubled about many things.

42 But one thing is needed, and Mary has chosen that good part, which will not be taken away from her."

Martha was "distracted" from the presence of the Lord due to her "much serving" (v. 40). Let's examine Martha for a moment:

- Martha received or welcomed Jesus (v. 38)
- Martha served the Lord (v. 40)
- Martha "prayed" to the Lord (v. 40), although it was mostly self-serving

I am sure that Martha loved the Lord, but she could not see the value of what seemed to be "doing nothing." Martha's approach left her with lots of worries and troubles. How would she get it all done? There were not enough people to help! It actually left her feeling like the Lord didn't care: "Do You not care that my sister has left me to serve alone?" Martha's approach reminds me of many pastors who are burnt out with the rigors of the ministry. But listen to what Jesus said to Martha. He said to her that Mary had "chosen" the good part – sitting at His feet and hearing His Word.

The power to serve was in the approach that Mary had taken. She *chose* to spend time with Jesus. The 100 church planters differentiated themselves from all of the others by also choosing the good part.

The man of God cannot make up in the flesh what can only be accomplished in the Spirit. There is absolutely too much spiritual warfare in the ministry to even attempt to succeed without the covering of His presence. God is looking for *Vertical Pastors* to lead His flock. Martha would be considered horizontal in her service to the Lord and Mary, vertical. Pastors, too easy, fall into the trap being everything to everybody and forfeiting time with God in the process.

When I wake up in the morning a little before 5:00am, I spend a few moments thanking the Lord for His presence and all that He will do for me that day. I then spend about an hour meditating in the Word. Next, I shower and dress and drive to the church for at least an hour of prayer. It is now close to 8:00am and I am ready to start my day, fueled up in the presence of God. More time in the Word and prayer flows throughout the day.

There are also seasons in our lives and ministries when the Lord will call us unto Himself. When I was first saved and called into the ministry. God separated me unto Him with prayer and the Word. For a period of almost five years, I spend five hours a day studying the Word and three hours a day praying. I also spent extended periods of days fasting before the Lord. At the end of this season, God sent me to Bible College. However, my true education came at the feet of Jesus in the "school of the Holy Spirit."

When Jesus called the twelve disciples, take note of their first calling:

> **Mark 3:**
> **13 And He went up on the mountain and called to Him those He Himself wanted. And they came to Him.**
> **14 Then He appointed twelve, that they might be with Him and that He might send them out to preach,**

15 and to have power to heal sicknesses and to cast out demons.

The first and highest calling of the twelve was "that they might be **with Him**." The order of our Lord's calling never changes:

1. Be with Him
2. Preach the Word
3. Minister healing and deliverance

The Lord Himself knew that He could not bypass time with the Father before ministering to the needs of the people.

> **Mark 1:**
> **35 Now in the morning, having risen a long while before daylight, He went out and departed to a solitary place; and there He prayed.**
> **36 And Simon and those who were with Him searched for Him.**
> **37 When they found Him, they said to Him, "Everyone is looking for You."**

The disciples were concerned with all of the needs that were present with the large crowd that was gathering. Jesus knew that without the power of the Holy Spirit nothing life-changing could be accomplished. This power came through time of prayer and communion with God. Jesus put the vertical on priority in order to meet the needs of the horizontal.

If you remember our section on deacons, the whole reason for the office of deacons was that the apostles could spend more time in prayer and the Word.

Acts 6:
2 Then the twelve summoned the multitude of the disciples and said, "It is not desirable that we should leave the word of God and serve tables.
3 Therefore, brethren, seek out from among you seven men of good reputation, full of the Holy Spirit and wisdom, whom we may appoint over this business;
4 but we will give ourselves continually to prayer and to the ministry of the word."

The vertical pastor must give himself continually to prayer and the ministry of the Word. This is one of the main reasons that the church needs the ministries of elders and deacons. One may ask, if the pastor is spending most of his time praying and studying God's Word, how will the church ever grow? Doesn't he need to be out beating the bushes for new members and visiting the existing members? To answer that question, let's read what happened to the early church in response to the actions taken in Acts chapter 6:

Acts 6:7 Then the word of God spread, and the number of the disciples multiplied greatly in Jerusalem, and a great many of the priests were obedient to the faith.

As a result of the apostles going vertical, the church began to grow greatly. The church will enjoy much greater victory when the man of God is standing in the gap for the people before the Lord. In the early days of a church plant, it may be necessary for the pastor to spend more time in horizontal ministry (much like the apostles until the church exponentially grew). However, as the body grows and people are placed into leadership positions, the paradigm should shift and reflect more time in the vertical role than the horizontal one. If I were to place a percentage on the time spent between the two, it would only be a general guideline, as there are numerous variables. However, for the purpose of generating thought, I recommend that in an established church, that the split be 70% vertical and 30% horizontal.

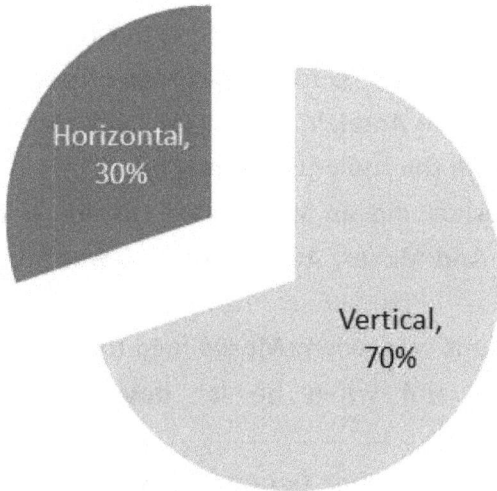

Below are some examples of the vertical and horizontal aspects of ministry:

Vertical	Horizontal
• Prayer	• Counseling
• Worship	• Visitation
• Studying the Word	• Church functions
• Meditating in the Word	• Business meetings
• Sermon preparation	• Physical labor

The one area of ministry that is a hybrid of the two is preaching under the anointing of the Holy Spirit and ministering in the gifts of the Spirit. While the one being used is ministering horizontally to the needs of the people, at the same time, he is being ministered to by the Holy Spirit.

Do you remember when Israel was in battle against the Amalekites and Moses was on the hill with his arms raised? God's people prevailed when his arms were raised and when he let his arms down, the enemy prevailed.

> **Exodus 17:**
> **8 Now Amalek came and fought with Israel in Rephidim.**
> **9 And Moses said to Joshua, "Choose us some men and go out, fight with Amalek. Tomorrow I will stand on the top of the hill with the rod of God in my hand."**
> **10 So Joshua did as Moses said to him, and fought with Amalek. And Moses, Aaron, and Hur went up to the top of the hill.**
> **11 And so it was, when Moses held up his hand, that Israel prevailed; and when he let down his hand, Amalek prevailed.**
> **12 But Moses' hands became heavy; so they took a stone and put it under him, and he sat on it. And Aaron and Hur supported his hands, one on one side, and the other on the other side; and his hands were steady until the going down of the sun.**
> **13 So Joshua defeated Amalek and his people with the edge of the sword.**

This story of the battle between Israel and Amalek illustrates the importance of this book's content. When Moses, the man of God over the people, held up his hands, Israel prevailed. But when he became weary and he let his hands down, Amalek prevailed. But victory was secured when Aaron and Hur, types of the ministry of elders and deacons, supported the hands of Moses until the going down of the sun.

It is my prayer that every leader reading this book will find their place in God's plan. Whether you are a five-fold leader, an elder or a deacon, spend time with God and get His perfect will for your life. These are the last days. God desires to fill His house with His glory.

We must line up to His Word, not just with outward observance, but with the heart and attitude.

Study Questions: Section Four

1. What are the two words used for "feed" in John 21:15-17? What are their definitions and their significance?

_____

_____

_____

2. What is the primary type of shepherding for five-fold elders? What is the primary type of shepherding for supportive elders?

Five-fold:

_____

_____

Supportive:

_____

_____

3. What are some of the negative characteristics of sheep?

_____

_____

_____

_____

4. What are some of the positive characteristics of sheep?

_____

_____

_____

_____

5. Name some of the ways that sheep and goats are opposites.

_____

_____

_____

6. Should a shepherd leave the sheep to go retrieve a goat? Why?

_____

_____

7. How can sheep protect themselves from a wolf that enters the fold? What type of sheep is an easy prey?

_____

_____

8. Name some of the characteristics of a wolf.

_____

_____

_____

_____

9. Describe the work of a sheep dog. How does it relate to the role of elders?

_____

_____

_____

_____

10. What are some of the qualities one needs to be a good sheep dog?

_____

_____

_____

11. Describe the difference between Martha's and Mary's ministry.

_____

_____

_____

_____

12. What was the first and highest calling of the apostles?

_____

_____

13. Describe the difference between vertical and horizontal ministry. Provide examples.

_____

_____

_____

_____

_____

_____

14. What is a good guideline to use for percentage time spent between vertical and horizontal ministry?

_____

_____

15. How does the example of Moses on the hill relate to church life and the role of elders and deacons?

_____

_____

_____

_____

Personal Evaluation

Please answer the following questions honestly and objectively. If this is to be used for evaluation by a pastor, the information will be kept confidential.

1. Describe your salvation experience; your Holy Spirit baptism experience.

Salvation:

_____

_____

_____

Holy Spirit:

_____

_____

_____

2. How long have you been at your present church? What is your present relationship with your pastor(s)?

_____

_____

_____

3. How many churches have you been a part of the last ten years? On what terms have you left each of those churches? May your previous pastors be contacted concerning this information?

_____

_____

_____

_____

4. What are your personal goals and ministry goals?

Personal:

_____

_____

Ministry:

_____

_____

5. Do you feel called to a five-fold ministry? Explain.

_____

_____

_____

_____

6. Which of the two offices covered in this book do you feel best suited for: elder or deacon? Why?

_____

_____

_____

_____

7. Do you feel that you meet with the qualifications found in I Timothy 3:1-12 and Titus 1:6-9? Explain why or why not.

_____

_____

_____

_____

8. From the lists of qualifications for elders and deacons, list what you consider to be your major strengths.

_____

_____

_____

9. From the same lists of qualifications, list what you consider to be your major weaknesses.

_____

_____

_____

10. What are your personal views on submission to authority?

_____

_____

_____

11. If you disagreed with a decision that your pastor(s) made, how would you handle it and could you still submit from your heart and support that decision (given that it was not morally, ethically or doctrinally wrong)?

_____

_____

_____

_____

12. Have you ever been removed from a leadership position? If so, what position and why?

_____

_____

_____

13. What person has had the greatest influence on your walk with God and why?

_____

_____

_____

14. How many times have you been married? Give the circumstances surrounding any divorces (e.g., how long ago, before or after saved, adultery involved, lessons learned, etc.).

_____

_____

_____

15. Which of the following describes your marriage?

☐ Happy and in divine order according to Ephesians 5:22-33.
☐ Up and down and not completely in divine order.
☐ Unhappy and completely out of divine order.

Explain:

_____

_____

_____

16. Does your wife meet with the qualifications for elder's and deacon's wives as found in I Timothy 3:11? If not, where does she lack?

_____

_____

_____

17. Which of the following describes your children's attitude?

☐ Very respectful and submissive toward their parents and the things of God.
☐ Somewhat respectful and submissive toward their parents and the things of God.
☐ Disrespectful and unsubmissive toward their parents and the things of God.

Explain:

_____

_____

_____

18. Please give a brief description of your employment history.

_____

_____

_____

_____

_____

19. What, if any, formal Bible training have you had?

_____

_____

_____

20. Please list ten doctrines which you consider to be essential to the faith.
1. _____
2. _____
3. _____
4. _____
5. _____
6. _____
7. _____
8. _____
9. _____
10. _____

21. Which of the following describes your daily time in prayer?

☐ 15 to 30 minutes
☐ 30 minutes to one hour
☐ One to two hours
☐ More than two hours

22. Have you ever operated in any of the nine gifts of the Spirit (I Cor. 12:7-10)? If so, which ones and how frequent?

_____

_____

_____

_____

23. Examine the list of motivational gifts found in Romans 12:6-8 and identify the one(s) that you have. Also list any other gifts, talents or abilities which you have that could be a source of edification to the church.

_____

_____

_____

_____

24. What areas of the book did you disagree with? Why?

_____

_____

_____

_____

25. Why do you want to be in a position of leadership?

_____

_____

_____

_____